Sartre's Concept of a Person

University of Massachusetts Press Amherst   1976

Sartre's Concept of a Person:

An Analytic Approach

by Phyllis Sutton Morris

Copyright © 1975 by
The University of Massachusetts Press
All rights reserved
Library of Congress Catalog Card Number 75-8451
ISBN 0-87023-185-5
Printed in the United States of America

Publication of this book was assisted by the
American Council of Learned Societies under a grant
from the Andrew W. Mellon Foundation.

Library of Congress Cataloging in Publication Data

Morris, Phyllis Sutton, 1931–
    Sartre's concept of a person.

    A revision of the author's thesis, University of
Michigan, 1969.
    Bibliography: p.
    Includes index.
    1. Sartre, Jean Paul, 1905–   2. Personality.
I. Title.
B2430.S34M65 1975 126'.092'4 75-8451
ISBN 0-87023-185-5

for two Johns:

late father
early husband

Contents

Preface

While I hope that this book will be of interest to Sartre's many admirers, one of my main concerns has been to open Sartre's work to a new audience, which has been, to this point, relatively hostile to his ideas when it has taken them at all seriously.

For the English-speaking analytic philosopher, the central problem in trying to understand Sartre is not that he is a French philosopher writing in French, for most of Sartre's important early works are available in translation. Rather, one of the severest difficulties is that, even in English, Sartre's ideas are obscured by his strange and difficult terminology. Most of the literature on Sartre merely paraphrases him without clarifying what he means. Another common difficulty has been that commentators have frequently tried to discuss too many of Sartre's ideas in too little space, with the result that Sartre's claims are not made clear.

To avoid both of these problems, I thought it might make sense if this study were limited to a relatively small number of points in Sartre's position, and if the attempt were made to render these points and the supporting arguments as precisely and as thoroughly as possible.

It should be clear from this procedure that the scope of this study is limited. It is not intended to be a definitive account of all of Sartre's ideas, but rather a clear and thorough account of that segment of Sartre's early writings that pertains to an analysis of his concept of a person. This subject was chosen in part because it has been little discussed by his English-speaking commentators, in part because his treatment of the concept of a person includes many questions discussed by contemporary English-speaking philosophers, and in part because it seems to be a sound, central, and extremely important part of his position, the clarification of which should illuminate many other elements of his work.

The hope of making sense out of Sartre's ideas for the analytically oriented English-speaking philosopher has influenced several points of method. In most of the ensuing discussion I have started by asking certain questions that are discussed among analytic philosophers. Sartre's position with respect to these questions has been reconstructed from discussions scattered throughout his early writings. There is, of course, a danger of misinterpretation in taking points from one context and inserting them into a new context. However, this method can provide a fresh and illuminating approach to understanding these points. I have made every effort to avoid distorting Sartre's position, although, as I have noted on occasion, it has been necessary to try to fill in some gaps.

Another decision that has been in part influenced by the hope of communicating with the English-speaking reader is the decision to deal only with Sartre's early works, most of which are available in English translation. Those readers familiar with Sartre's later work, in particular his *Critique de la Raison Dialectique*, may find it odd that I do not undertake to show the development of Sartre's position through time. However, since this book is not yet available in translation, except for the preface, the audience I am most concerned to address has not yet offered serious criticisms of it.

Another important reason for this decision, however, is that I wanted to show the basic coherence of that early position, which is so often ignored, misunderstood, or abused as incoherent by his critics. I did not see a good way of showing this coherence in detail while, at the same time, taking into account the sharp changes in direction which Sartre's thinking underwent soon after the publication of *Being and Nothingness*. His early concern for an analysis of the structures of individual consciousness, which is closely connected with our topic, was later replaced by an emphasis on social and political questions. His thinking on freedom and on man's relation to the physical world shifted in his later writing. The interested reader may want to look at Hazel Barnes' new book, *Sartre*, which includes a lucid and sympathetic account of Sartre's development.

There is another gap in my treatment which needs to be mentioned. There has been no attempt to trace the historical connections between Sartre's work and the work of Heidegger, Husserl, and Hegel. These connections have been discussed by some of Sartre's English-speaking commentators, and it seemed pointless to duplicate their efforts. For instance, Sartre's indebtedness to the German thinkers with respect to his solution to the problem of other minds has been pointed out by Mary Warnock, Klaus Hartmann, Marjorie Grene, and Wilfred Desan, among others. Also, since the basic need is clarification, it seemed to make more sense to compare Sartre's position to the views of English-speaking philosophers rather than to the ideas of German thinkers, who are not well known to most American and English philosophers.

It has been customary to interpret Sartre as one who follows the rationalist tradition. This line of interpretation is continued in two recent works which I read too late to respond to in detail in this work: Marjorie Grene's *Sartre* and Hazel Barnes' *Sartre*. The professional philosopher may be puzzled at times to discover that the claim that Sartre is a rationalist is sometimes presented in such a way as to suggest merely that he is not irrational. I have no quarrel with such a claim, except to point out that philosophers usually contrast rationalism to empiricism rather than to irrationalism. Grene takes the more traditional view of rationalism when she interprets Sartre as a neo-Cartesian.

I do not think that Sartre is wholly free of rationalist elements; his opposition to the atomistic empiricist account of perception is enough to rouse suspicions. But, after all, there may be very few pure rationalists or pure empiricists since Kant. In any case, what has made me most uncomfortable about the usual interpretation of Sartre as a rationalist *simpliciter* is that rationalism has traditionally espoused the doctrines of an immaterial substantial ego and innate ideas. Sartre attacks both of these positions, and espouses alternatives which can be compared with traditional empiricist solutions, as I try to show. In his history of the phenomenological movement, Herbert Spiegelberg suggested that it might be fruitful to clarify the connections between that movement and the mainstream of empiricism. This study has taken its inspiration in part from that suggestion.

In the ensuing discussion I would like to offer support for the following claims: (a) that Sartre's early analysis of the concept of a person is basically coherent. (Sometimes his terminology obscures this point; he argues that the concept of a person is ambiguous, but he offers a consistent treatment of that ambiguity) (b) that Sartre's discussion is addressed to, and sheds light on, many of the questions discussed by contemporary analytic philosophers; and (c) that Sartre's analysis of the concept of a person raises some philosophically interesting new questions.

An early version of my book was presented to the University of Michigan in 1969 in the form of a doctoral dissertation.

University of Michigan scholarships during the years 1966/67 and 1967/68 were instrumental in permitting me to complete most of the original research and writing of that thesis. I owe a special debt of gratitude for inspiration and encouragement to Professor Frithjof H. Bergmann, who chaired my thesis committee. In addition, Professors William Frankena, Julius Moravcsik, and Jack Meiland made especially helpful detailed comments on that thesis.

A paper based on my dissertation was read at the Western Division meeting of the American Philosophical Association in May 1969. A slightly revised version of that paper, on Sartre's resolution of the problem of other minds, was published in *The Journal of the British Society for Phenomenology*, volume 1, number 2, May 1970. I am grateful to the editor of that journal, Dr. Wolfe Mays, for his kind permission to use material from that article in the present work. My chapter on character reflects some of the comments made by those who heard a paper I read to the Creighton Club in October 1969.

I am deeply grateful to the Board of Trustees of Kirkland College for the award of a research professorship which released me from teaching duties and enabled me to work full time in research and revision of my dissertation during the spring semester of 1971. I appreciate the release from committee responsibilities during that semester and encouragement offered by President Samuel F. Babbitt of Kirkland College.

I acknowledge, with thanks, the excellent suggestions and criticisms offered by numerous people. Professors Norman E. Bowie, Adele Laslie, Anthony Manser, John M. Morris, Robert Simon, and Richard Taylor commented critically on my discussion of other minds, as did Kenneth C. Heisler and L. E. Sternberg. Professor Gary Cox offered critical comments on my discussion of character. I am indebted to Professor David A. Begelman for some challenging discussions of B. F. Skinner. Needless to say, any mistakes which remain are my own. I am grateful to the National Endowment for the Humanities for enabling me to participate in one of their summer seminars in 1974. Some of the material on Freud and on Sartre's concept of self-deception was based on research conducted during that seminar.

I wish to thank Mrs. Bonnie Bowie for the speed and accuracy with which she typed my manuscript. To my husband John and to my children, William and Katherine, I owe thanks for their sustained assistance and encouragement.

Introduction

This study will develop an interpretation of Sartre's concept of a person. Two topics of interest to contemporary English-speaking philosophers provide the main focus: criteria of identity for persons and the question of the existence of other minds. Three criteria of identity have been widely discussed; bodily identity, memory, and character. Sartre discusses all of these, and has added a fourth criterion.

The tradition of considering persons as moral agents goes back at least as far as Locke. A great deal of the contemporary discussion, although not all of it, emphasizes epistemological considerations; that is, it deals with persons as perceivers. Sartre's discussion places emphasis on persons as moral agents. The traditional questions of individuation and reidentification of persons are given some attention and placed within the context of their connection to moral practice. Sartre is more deeply concerned, however, with establishing the differences between persons and material objects; that is, he asks how X can be identified as a person rather than, say, as a corpse or a cleverly devised robot.

Each of these questions can be asked from the point of view of the person himself or from the point of view of others who identify him. At certain stages in the discussion, this difference in viewpoint becomes important for Sartre's position.

The questions may be seen as very closely connected or as sharply distinguishable, depending on what position is being defended. For instance, someone who defends certain extreme forms of physicalism or behaviorism might argue that there is no essential difference between human beings and other physical organisms, and that therefore criteria for reidentification and for individuation of persons are the same as for any other living physical thing. But if one were to give a quite different answer to the third question, and hold, for instance, that persons are the sort of entities which could exist apart from the original body, the first two questions require special consideration. One could no longer rely on wholly physical criteria for reidentification of such entities, for it might be the case that the person has changed to another body. Nor could one rely on wholly physical criteria for individuation of persons, for two persons might coexist in a single body. It should be apparent that serious conceptual difficulties can arise, with respect to our customary practices of locating persons responsible for actions and punishing guilty persons, if persons are conceived as separable from their bodies.

Sartre defends the claim that there are sharp differences between human beings and physical objects; and it may be helpful to ask why he does. With increasing emphasis on the authority of the sciences during this century, there has been a corresponding increase in the emphasis on human beings as products of natural law. One result of scientific activity has been to obliterate or minimize whatever differences there are between persons and material objects. This has not been a universal result, of course. Even a physicalist or a behaviorist may insist that there are important differences between human beings and other kinds of physical objects.

One extreme position has developed, however, and it is this position that Sartre is especially concerned to attack. It is possible to maintain that persons are not basically different from other material objects and, at the same time, that persons can and should be held responsible for actions they have performed. Sartre does not criticize this position. On the other hand, the claim that there is no basic distinction between persons and material objects can lead, and has led, to the further claim that persons are not responsible for their actions. In the latter case, the point seems to be that since conditions beyond the control of the individual determine his actions, it would make as little sense to treat a person as an accountable moral agent as it would to treat earthquakes or preying hawks as morally responsible for the effects they produce. Sartre does not attack determinism in general. He does, however, attack a version of psychological determinism which he thinks would lead to the view that persons are not responsible. This is discussed later.

One of the basic reasons, then, for Sartre's emphasis on the distinction between persons and material objects is to provide an alternative to this strain in modern science and philosophy. A dual purpose might be said to underlie Sartre's concept of a person. First, he wants to defend the claim that persons are morally responsible agents. Second, he wants to achieve this without taking one of the traditional routes for doing it. That is, he does not want to defend the position that there are, in addition to bodies, immaterial spiritual subjects which are responsible for actions.

The details of Sartre's attempt to fulfill these purposes provide the substance of this book. My interpretation is based on the assumption that there are two fundamental mainsprings of Sartre's idea of the person as moral agent: the concept of intentionality and the claim that "I" is ambiguous. Sartre's position is reconstructed within the framework of an analysis of these two central notions. Some of the limitations of Sartre's position will also be spelled out.

Chapter 1

Intentionality and the Reducibility Thesis

In at least one respect, persons may be physical objects, or have some characteristics of physical objects. Persons are thought to be, in part, bodies, or to have, among other characteristics, bodily qualities. One of the central controversies in the recent literature on personal identity centers on the connection between persons and their bodies. It is sometimes asserted, sometimes denied, that there is a logical connection between persons and their bodies.

At least three separate issues have been discussed under this general heading, and it is important to distinguish them in order to make sense of Sartre's position. In general, what seems to be at issue is whether a person (or mind, or experience, or consciousness) is or is not logically separable from a given body, or from bodies in general. In particular, these three questions have been raised:

a) Whether descriptions of mental phenomena can be reduced without remainder into statements about physical objects and physical processes
b) Whether it is logically possible that persons (or minds, etc.) could exist separately from bodies in general or from the original body in particular
c) Whether there is a logical connection between mental phenomena, such as "experiences," and observable states of the body and its behavior

The three questions are related, and might become indistinguishable at times. Despite the close connection, however, they have been discussed in different contexts in the recent literature. Question (a) has been discussed in connection with attempts to distinguish between persons and material objects. Question (b) has traditionally been discussed in connection with the question of immortality, and recently in connection with the change-of-body thesis. Question (c) has been part of the discussion of the problem of other minds. Since different considerations are pertinent to these contexts, the questions will be distinguished in the present work.

Sartre's position can be characterized briefly with reference to these three questions and then developed in more detail. With regard to (a), Sartre denies the reducibility thesis. In particular, he claims that one characteristic of conscious human experience and action serves to distinguish conscious phenomena from wholly physical phenomena, and that its description cannot be reduced to the description of material processes: intentionality. This is the subject of the present chapter.

With regard to (b), Sartre denies that it makes sense to say that something mental or conscious can exist apart from bodies in general or from the original body in particular. Concerning (c), Sartre affirms the logical connection between experiences and observable behavior in one sense, but denies it in another sense. These claims, with their supporting arguments, will be discussed in later chapters.

Intentionality: Two Theses

One way of asking how persons are to be distinguished from physical objects has been to ask whether descriptions of conscious phenomena can be reduced without remainder into statements about physical objects and physical processes. For Sartre, the primary reason for denying the reducibility thesis is that human consciousness is intentional, while nonconscious things are not intentional.[1] In this chapter an attempt will be made to clarify what Sartre means by the term "intentionality," and to formulate three versions of his argument against the reducibility thesis. Since Roderick Chisholm's discussions of intentionality are familiar to English-speaking philosophers, it will be convenient to reconstruct Sartre's position by comparing it, at certain points, with claims defended by Chisholm.

Chisholm also uses the concept of intentionality to establish a distinction between the psychological and the nonpsychological; in this way he attempts to show that persons cannot be understood in solely physicalist terms.[2] The point is one that

1. Jean-Paul Sartre, *Being and Nothingness: An Essay on Phenomenological Ontology*, trans. Hazel E. Barnes (New York: Philosophical Library, 1956), pp. 85, 257, 289. Subsequent references to this work will be noted parenthetically in the text and abbreviated *BN*.
2. Roderick Chisholm, "On Some Psychological Concepts and the

both Sartre and Chisholm got from Brentano: Sartre indirectly, via Husserl, and Chisholm directly.[3]

Chisholm, in a discussion of intentionality, quotes the following passage from Franz Brentano's *Psychologie vom empirischen Standpunkt* (1874):

> Every mental phenomenon is characterized by what the scholastics of the Middle Ages called the intentional (and also mental) inexistence of an object, and what we would call, although not in entirely unambiguous terms, the reference to a content, a direction upon an object (by which we are not to understand a reality . . .), or an immanent objectivity. Each one includes something as an object within itself, although not always in the same way. In presentation something is presented, in judgment something is affirmed or denied, in love [something is] loved, in hate [something] is hated, in desire something is desired, etc.
>
> This intentional inexistence is exclusively characteristic of mental phenomena. No physical phenomenon manifests anything similar. Consequently, we can define mental phenomena by saying that they are such phenomena as include an object intentionally within themselves. [Vol. I, book II, ch. 1][4]

What, then, does it mean to say that conscious acts or processes are intentional? One reply, given at times by many philosophers, including both Sartre and Chisholm, is that consciousness refers to objects, or that a psychological act is about something. Chisholm, for instance, has said that "thoughts (i.e. beliefs, desires, etc.) are intentional—they are about some-

'Logic' of Intentionality," in *Intentionality, Minds and Perception*, ed. Hector-Neri Castañeda (Detroit: Wayne State University Press, 1967), p. 12. Hereafter cited as "Some Psychological Concepts."

3. Roderick M. Chisholm, *Perceiving: A Philosophical Study* (Ithaca, N.Y.: Cornell University Press, 1957), p. 168. Also Roderick M. Chisholm, "Editor's Introduction," *Realism and the Background of Phenomenology*, Library of Philosophical Movements (New York: The Free Press, 1960; London: Collier-Macmillan, 1960), pp. 4, 17.

Jean-Paul Sartre, "Une Idée fondamentale de la phénoménologie de Husserl: L'intentionnalité," in *Situations I* (Paris: Gallimard, 1947). Hereafter cited as "L'intentionnalité." Joseph P. Fell's translation of this article appears in *Journal of the British Society for Phenomenology*, 1, no. 2 (May 1970): 4–5.

4. Roderick M. Chisholm, "Intentionality," in *Encyclopedia of Philosophy*, ed. Paul Edwards (8 vols.; New York: Macmillan & The Free Press, 1967; London: Collier-Macmillan, 1967), 4:201.

thing."[5] Sartre said "the profound meaning of the *cogito* is essentially to refer outside itself" (*BN*, 85). Reference has typically been considered one of the central characteristics of intentionality.

However, Brentano had said that one cannot speak in an "entirely unambiguous" manner of "reference to a content" or "direction upon an object." In some cases, a question has arisen over the use of the term "reference" when there is not, or may not be, an actually existing object. The point, apparently, is that there is reluctance to speak of reference when the existence of a referent is in doubt, since "reference," like the term "know," can be understood in a strong sense.[6] One move was to maintain, as Brentano did in the passage quoted, that there is an intentional object "immanent" in consciousness which could provide a referent in such cases. It is the peculiar nature of the intentional object, rather than reference *per se*, that has been central to most of Chisholm's discussions of intentionality.

In an article published in 1967, Chisholm distinguished quite sharply between two different theses of intentionality. There was an "ontological thesis" of intentionality, which took its point of departure from the nature of the intentional object; there was also a "psychological thesis" of intentionality, which implied that consciousness, unlike physical objects, is basically referential. Brentano linked the two theses in his early writings, but because of certain difficulties inherent in the notion of an intentional object, Chisholm says that Brentano later abandoned the ontological thesis of intentionality.[7]

Chisholm's discussions of intentionality appear to have undergone a similar evolution. In a number of discussions he has attempted to develop criteria for intentional statements which would imply neither the existence nor the nonexistence of the intentional object. Chisholm has used the "noninference criterion" repeatedly as a test of whether or not a statement could be counted as an intentional one, and has produced a variety of logical criteria designed to incorporate the noninference crite-

5. Roderick M. Chisholm, "Chisholm-Sellars Correspondence on Intentionality," in *Minnesota Studies in the Philosophy of Science, Vol. II: Concepts, Theories and the Mind-Body Problem*, ed. Herbert Feigl, Michael Scriven, and Grover Maxwell (Minneapolis: University of Minnesota Press, 1958), p. 533.

6. See Willard Van Orman Quine, *Word and Object* (Cambridge, Mass.: M.I.T. Press, 1960), p. 219. Quine speaks here of intentional statements as nonreferential. Also see Chisholm, "Intentionality," p. 202.

7. Chisholm, "Intentionality," pp. 201–2.

rion into intentional statements.[8] But there are at least two different answers to the question of what Chisholm has used this as a criterion for.

In his introduction to *Realism and the Background of Phenomenology*, for instance, Chisholm did not distinguish the two theses of intentionality, and he used the noninference criterion in connection with both.[9] In some of his more recent discussions, however, Chisholm has taken the noninference criterion to be connected with the psychological thesis of intentionality only, not with the combined ontological and psychological theses, as he did formerly. Chisholm did not reject the ontological thesis outright, but he came to consider it "problematic."[10]

The psychological thesis of intentionality, then, may be either linked to or dissociated from the ontological thesis that there are intentional objects which are, in some sense, "included within" mental phenomena. The fact that these two theses may be either linked or dissociated accounts for some of the differences of position with regard to the psychological thesis itself.

Sartre takes intentionality, initially in the sense of reference to an object, to be the distinguishing characteristic of consciousness. Nonconscious things are not intentional; they do not refer or "point beyond themselves." (Sartre takes a particular characteristic of reference as being of central importance, as we will see.) But Sartre combines the psychological thesis of intentionality, that reference to an object is (in part) what distinguishes conscious phenomena from purely physical phenomena, with a rejection of the other thesis. It is, in fact, in part *as* an attack on the ontological thesis of intentionality that Sartre supports Husserl's view that "all consciousness is consciousness *of* something."[11]

Sartre's reasons for rejecting the ontological thesis of intentionality are directed against two supposed functions of in-

8. Richard Schmitt uses the expression "noninference criterion," in "Phenomenology," *Encyclopedia of Philosophy*, 6:145.

9. Chisholm, "Editor's Introduction," *Realism and the Background of Phenomenology*, p. 4.

10. Roderick M. Chisholm, "Brentano on Descriptive Psychology and the Intentional," in *Phenomenology and Existentialism*, ed. Edward N. Lee and Maurice Mandelbaum (Baltimore: Johns Hopkins Press, 1967), pp. 6, 20—22. Hereafter referred to as "Brentano."

11. Sartre, "L'intentionnalité," p. 33. Herbert Spiegelberg points out that Sartre, in this article, mistakenly believes Husserl's doctrine of intentionality implies that the referent exists independently of consciousness (*The Phenomenological Movement: A Historical Introduction* [2 vols., 2d ed.; The Hague: Martinus Nijhoff, 1969] 2:488).

tentional objects. One of these, already mentioned, is that the intentional object is supposed to be able to provide a referent in cases where there is not, or may not be, an existing referent. Another major function of the intentional object has been to provide what Chisholm calls a "literal interpretation" of the correspondence theory of truth. That is, a true statement is one which correctly affirms that the characteristics of the intentional object are "the same as those of the actual object."[12]

Sartre has pointed out that the notion of an immanent intentional object is superfluous, if its function is conceived in the way just described by Chisholm. In discussing the notion of a "sensation" or sense datum (i.e., an immanent object in consciousness which is supposed to "represent" some real object outside of consciousness), Sartre points out that we could not make a judgment whether or not there is such a correspondence or "representation" unless we first presupposed that we could directly see the real object. But if what we sense is the real object, there is no need for an extra, immanent object in consciousness. Sartre's objection is made in the context of a discussion of a psychological experiment, in which the assumption is made that the experimenter has direct access to perceptual data concerning the subject's reactions and instrument readings, while the further assumption is made that the subject himself is producing subjective visual "representations" which give him only indirect access to objects perceived (*BN*, 311–15).[13] The conceptual flaw in the experimenter's position is one that Sartre sees as derived from a philosophical mistake.

Chisholm claims, in the passage just mentioned, that one main advantage of the doctrine of intentional inexistence is to provide a "literal interpretation" for the correspondence theory of truth. Many of Sartre's arguments against the doctrine of immanence are directed against the claim that intentional objects could have the same properties as real objects which are outside of or "transcendent" to consciousness. This claim cannot be taken literally without incurring one of several unacceptable results, Sartre maintains.

For instance, one way of making the claim that intentional

12. Chisholm, "Intentionality," p. 201. Here Chisholm is considering difficulties in this position, not defending it.

13. Cf. the similar criticism made of the psychologist's position by E. B. Holt et al. in "Introduction to *The New Realism*," in *Realism and the Background of Phenomenology*, p. 182; also Chisholm, "Intentionality," p. 201.

objects have the same properties as real objects would be to say that intentional objects possess the spatial and other character-istics of physical objects. If the immanent tree is to be viewed as a "true representation" of the real tree, within the literal correspondence theory mentioned by Chisholm, it would have to possess the same properties as the real tree. But the real tree possesses the properties of being outside me, twisted and alone in the dust at the side of the road. If the intentional object had these properties, it could not "enter into" consciousness; it would not *be* an immanent object. On the other hand, if it does not possess these properties, it does not correspond in a literal way to the real tree.[14]

The idealist position, as Sartre views it, commits the opposite error. Instead of making "contents" of consciousness physical in nature, it reduces physical objects to a certain combination and order of contents of consciousness. The idealist reduction-ism which dissolves the apparent solidity and spatiality of physical objects into a "sluggish fog" (*"un brouillard mou"*) makes solipsism inevitable.[15]

Another possibility, Sartre says, would be to say that there are immanent objects which possess the contradictory qualities of both consciousness and physical objects: "contents" of con-sciousness become inert-living, exterior-interior, passive-active. Whichever of these moves is made, the doctrine of the existence of intentional objects assumes that the "mind" is spatial; that is, it forms a container or "closed box" for holding the immanent contents of consciousness (*BN*, 313–14). This can be mentioned as one of the auxiliary assumptions of the ontological thesis of intentionality to which Sartre objected. He said that philosophy ought to be concerned at the outset to establish the "true connection" between consciousness and the world; to speak of consciousness as intentional is to say that it is "directed toward the outside" (*BN*, li, lii).

In raising these objections to the thesis that the properties of an intentional object might be the same as those of the real object, Sartre is taking the word "same" in a literal sense. It seems likely that a serious defender of the ontological thesis of

14. Sartre, "L'intentionnalité," p. 32.
15. Sartre, "L'intentionnalité," pp. 31–32. Cf. G. E. Moore, "The Refutation of Idealism," in *Philosophical Studies* (Totowa, N.J.: Little-field, Adams, 1965), pp. 26–29. Two moves Moore makes against solip-sism are to (a) distinguish between the content of sensation and an object of sensation, and (b) make awareness a relation to an object.

intentionality might disagree with Chisholm's claim that such a literal interpretation should be given to the term. An obvious move would be to interpret "sameness of properties" in a figurative or analogical sense. It is not at all clear that Sartre's arguments, which assume the literal sameness of properties of intentional and real objects, could be applied with equal force to a sophisticated analogical view.

For this reason, his earlier argument, that the intentional object is superfluous, seems to be more convincing; if the intentional object has no function to fulfill within the correspondence theory, it would not matter whether its properties were really the same or only figuratively the same as those of the real object. It would be unnecessary to posit this extra entity, the intentional object. On the other hand, if Chisholm is correct in thinking that the real advantage of the doctrine of intentional inexistence is to provide a literal interpretation of the correspondence theory, Sartre's additional arguments appear to be both relevant and correct.

Sartre's argument that the intentional object is unnecessary is directed against its supposed function in a correspondence theory of truth; in this case, it has been supposed that there is a really existing object in addition to the intentional object. It was pointed out earlier that another function of the doctrine of intentional inexistence was to provide a referent in cases where there was no actually existing object in addition to the intentional object. The problem here, Sartre claims, is that if the existence of an intentional object is posited in order to provide a referent in cases where there is no other existing referent, the very condition of being able to imagine is undermined. The intentional object is, in this role, again superfluous. While the act of imagining is a real act, it is just the fact that the object of such an act does not exist, or exists elsewhere, or is absent, or is not posited as existing at all, that *makes* it an imaginary object. It is because Peter is absent that I can imagine his face, instead of perceiving it; if he were here in my consciousness, why would I go looking for him? There is no need here, either, for an intentional object.[16]

Thus, in emphasizing the referential nature of consciousness, Sartre does not mean to imply the further thesis that inten-

16. Jean-Paul Sartre, *Psychology of the Imagination* (New York: Citadel Press, 1948), pp. 265–72. Chisholm discusses a similar objection; see his "Intentionality," pp. 201–2.

tional objects are immanent in consciousness. He offers reasons for rejecting both major functions of intentional objects. However, when he emphasizes the referential character of consciousness, and at the same time denies the ontological thesis of intentionality, Sartre does not mean that there can be consciousness of existing objects only. We can be aware of objects that exist, of objects that do not exist, and of objects that may or may not exist.[17]

Some philosophers would undoubtedly object to Sartre's claim that consciousness is referential in cases where there is not, or may not be, an existing referent. For Sartre, however, the question of whether or not the object of consciousness exists is not the main point of referentiality. Rather, what he wants to focus on here is a similarity of structure in all cases of "consciousness of x." Specifically, an act of consciousness exists as a kind of pointing beyond itself. It does not exist, that is, in the form of an entity which contains its own objects. Sartre uses varied terminology in making this claim; sometimes, for instance, he uses such terms as "surpassing" and "transcending" to mean "referring" (*BN*, 85, 294–95).[18] It is not the particular expression "reference," then, that Sartre wants to argue about.

In order to take account of the objection mentioned, however, a strong and a weak sense of "reference" can be distinguished. The strong sense of the term would be the sense in which an existing referent is implied. The weak sense, which is applicable to Sartre's position, will be used in the following cases: when there is an existing object, or an object that does not exist, or an object which may or may not exist. Weak reference is different from not referring at all; in the latter case, there is *no* object that can be mentioned, existing or otherwise. If there were no object at all, however, Sartre does not think we could speak of an act of consciousness (*BN*, 621).

The question now is to discover more precisely what Sartre thinks is the common structure underlying all instances of "consciousness of x." This will permit us to give a preliminary answer to the question of reducibility with which we began, and also to see why this part of Sartre's answer would be inadequate if taken alone.

17. Sartre, *Psychology of the Imagination,* p. 16.
18. Sartre also uses these terms in other senses.

The First Argument against Reducibility:
Intentionality as Reference

When Sartre says that human consciousness is intentional, primarily in the sense of referring to something or having an object, he means to contrast consciousness with things, or physical objects, which are not intentional, which do not refer to anything. It is this contrast which underlies some of Sartre's key terminology. In part because of its lack of reference to anything outside itself, Sartre uses the term *"en-soi,"* or "being-in-itself," when he speaks of the thing or physical object. The physical object exists as a complete thing: "in order to be, it needs only itself; it refers only to itself" (*BN*, 171). Consciousness, on the other hand, is incomplete without its object, a "lack"; it exists only in the form of consciousness *of* something (*BN*, li). Consciousness that could be complete in itself, that could lack an object, would be an "abstraction," Sartre contends (*BN*, 621).

The point that Sartre emphasizes repeatedly in such terms and phrases is that physical objects are complete; consciousness, on the other hand, is in principle incomplete in the sense of requiring an object of some sort. There is always, he says, a "necessity for consciousness to exist as consciousness of something other than itself."[19] The completeness-incompleteness contrast underlies many of Sartre's examples, as well as his terminology.

For example, Sartre considers whether clouds might be thought of as "referring to" or "being about" rain. He replies in the negative: the cloud is only a certain amount of water vapor which can be described in terms of its temperature and pressure (*BN*, 98). It requires a conscious human observer to look at the cloud formation and to see this object as "surpassing" or referring to a possibility of future rain. The cloud itself does not refer to future rain; the human prediction does.

In another example, Sartre says that a nerve can be described in great detail, but that it is merely a "colloidal substance"; it does not refer to anything outside itself, and "under no circumstances could the nerve furnish the basis for meaning" (*BN*, 560).

19. Sartre, "L'intentionnalité," p. 33: "... nécessité pour la conscience d'exister comme conscience d'autre chose que soi."

Again, a description of the physiological and anatomical structures of visual perception treats the body as a mere physical object or "corpse"; such a description, Sartre insists, cannot account for the fact that the act of perceiving an object requires an object not contained in the organism (*BN*, 348). Can't signs, billboards, and written words be taken as counterexamples? Aren't these cases of physical objects which refer? Sartre's reply to this is the same as Chisholm's to a similar question. Sentences refer, says Chisholm, only in the sense that people use them to refer. *Qua* physical objects, they do not refer at all.[20]

The initial argument that Sartre wishes to make against the reducibility thesis, if this interpretation of his terms and examples is correct, can be formulated as follows. It is impossible to reduce descriptions of conscious phenomena without remainder into statements about physical objects, because it is theoretically possible to give a complete description of a physical object and it is impossible in principle to give a complete description of an act of consciousness.

Sartre would admit that it might be very difficult in practice to produce a complete description of a physical object. The point, however, is that a physical object is an independently existing entity, that is, a substance; a full description of its qualities could be produced without the necessity of referring to anything outside the object itself. But one must always include an object outside of an act of consciousness in order to complete a description of that act. All consciousness is consciousness of _____. The blank must always be filled by something which is other than the act of consciousness in question.

Sartre makes the point in the following way: "The for-itself is in no way an autonomous substance." "Consciousness does not have by itself any sufficiency of being as an absolute subjectivity; from the start it refers to the thing" (*BN*, 618).

There are two claims here, and objections can be made against both. One claim is that an act of consciousness is basically incomplete, that it requires something other than itself in order to exist. Objection can be made that if consciousness could be seen to contain intentional objects within itself, it could be argued that consciousness is "complete" in just the sense that Sartre denies. A complete description of consciousness could be given without mentioning anything outside of consciousness, since its objects are—in some sense—"in" con-

20. Chisholm, "Some Psychological Concepts," p. 52. Cf. *BN*, p. 427: the exit sign, says Sartre, is a "humanized" object.

sciousness. For Sartre, the claim that consciousness is incomplete in relation to its objects rests on his objections to the view that there are intentional objects immanent in consciousness. These have already been discussed.

The second claim is that physical objects are substances, that is, independently existing entities, and that it is therefore theoretically possible to give a complete description of a physical object that does not refer to anything other than the object itself. It might be possible to attack this claim directly, but it does not appear to be necessary to dispute Sartre's point in any way to show that the reducibility thesis is untouched. The reason is as follows.

If one were to speak not of physical objects but of physical relations, a glaring difficulty emerges. The problem for Sartre is that the same claim could be made concerning purely physical relations that he makes for consciousness. If one grants Sartre's point that the Empire State Building is a substance, and that its complete description could be given, the same points do not hold true for the physical relation "the Empire State Building is taller than y." One could say of this relation, using Sartrean terminology, that it is a "lack," that it is incomplete by itself, and that no complete description of it can be given without referring to something other than the relation itself, namely, the y required as the second term of the physical relation.

The objection gains force when the explicit point is made that, for Sartre, consciousness or the *for-itself* is a relation. He says, "the for-itself makes known to itself what it is, through the in-itself; that is, from the fact that in its being it is a relation to being" (*BN*, 216). Again, "*the for-itself is relation*" (*BN*, 362). Still again, "the for-itself is a relation to the world" (*BN*, 306). Nothing has been said so far about the first term of that relation, nor whether weak reference can be considered to be a real relation. In the present context, the point is simply to emphasize the difficulty Sartre faces in his discussion of reference as the primary characteristic of intentionality.

In attacking the reducibility thesis, Sartre has maintained that reference to an object is a characteristic of consciousness which is not shared by physical phenomena. In portions of his discussion he has selected a particular property of the structure of reference, incompleteness in relation to an object, as the characteristic of statements about mental phenomena which could not be reduced to statements about physical phenomena. If my interpretation of Sartre's reasoning is correct thus far, his mistake is that incompleteness is not a unique property of consciousness but, rather, a unique property of *relations*, both physical and mental. His incompleteness criterion leaves the possibility that consciousness is a physical relation, if not a physical object.[21] The point is obscured in Sartre's discussion because he typically contrasts consciousness to physical things, rather than to physical relations. The latter would have produced a more balanced comparison, and it would have forced him to combine, in an explicit fashion, this part of his account of intentionality with another part of his account.

The question concerning reducibility must now be restated: What distinguishes physical relations from conscious relations?

The Second Argument against Reducibility: Intentionality as Purpose

In Sartre's view, the concept of intentionality is broader than, although it includes, the idea of reference. It also includes the idea of purpose (*BN*, 477). It has been shown why the idea of reference alone, analyzed as incompleteness in relation to a second term, will not permit Sartre to distinguish physical relations from mental relations. It is the second part of Sartre's concept of intentionality, that is, purpose, that enables Sartre to begin to make the further distinction he needs.

In the current literature there has been some discussion whether there is a connection between intentionality and intention *qua* purpose. Feigl, for example, distinguishes quite sharply between intention in the sense of reference and intention in the sense of purpose.[22] Chisholm at one point includes "purposing" among intentional attitudes, although it does not appear to occupy any special status.[23] Bruce Aune spells out the connection in a way that appears to be consistent with Chisholm's position; the former points out that intentions (purposes) involve some conception of what is intended, and also involve the agent's beliefs about the appropriate conditions for realization of some purpose. Beliefs and conceptions, as Aune points out,

21. Cf. Anthony Kenny, *Action, Emotion and Will* (London: Routledge & Kegan Paul; New York: Humanities Press, 1963), p. 195. Kenny notes that "cut" and "heat" both require objects, although they are not mental terms.

22. Herbert Feigl, "The 'Mental' and the 'Physical,'" *Minnesota Studies*, 2:417.

23. Chisholm, "Some Psychological Concepts," p. 33.

are among those mental phenomena which possess the "marks of intentionality," that is, meet the noninference criterion.[24]

Stuart Hampshire takes a much stronger view of the connection. He says there is no genuine distinction between intention in the sense of reference, an intention that forms part of an action, and intention in the sense of an "unexpressed thought" or feeling directed toward something. His reason for maintaining the strong connection is that there are innumerable ways of classifying any element in reality, and that the differentiation of objects of reference into kinds depends in part on the usefulness, in terms of human purposes, of any given system of classification.[25] Hampshire's position is similar to Sartre's. In fact, one of the major themes throughout the remainder of this work will be to show many of the ways in which, for Sartre, purpose is connected with reference to objects. In the present context, the main point is to indicate how Sartre tries to distinguish between conscious relations and physical relations.

There are reasons for interpreting Sartre as wanting to make the strong claim that all instances of conscious reference entail at least an implicit, if not explicit, reference to some end or purpose (*BN*, 126).[26] The reasons are complicated, and cannot be fully supported until much later. It will be necessary first to give an account of the role played by the fundamental project in all conscious acts, for instance, seeing-as and remembering-as.

A weaker claim can be offered now as Sartre's reason for rejecting the reducibility thesis. It was pointed out that in some of his discussions of intentionality Sartre appears to think that reference, analyzed as incompleteness in relation to an object, is a unique feature of consciousness which cannot be reduced to statements about physical objects. It was argued that the incompleteness criterion might permit Sartre to distinguish between consciousness and physical objects, but certainly would not enable him to make a distinction between conscious relations and physical relations. Sartre's initial way of making this further distinction is that, in the case of conscious relations, the second term may be nonexistent. In the case of physical relations, however, Sartre assumes that the second term must exist (*BN*, 477). If it is admitted that at least some conscious reference has

---

24. Bruce Aune, "Intention," *Encyclopedia of Philosophy*, 4:199.
25. Stuart Hampshire, *Thought and Action* (New York: Viking Press, 1960), pp. 19–21, 200–201.
26. The point should be emphasized that, for Sartre, there need not be explicit awareness of our ends. Not all of our purposing is *on* purpose, in other words.

a nonexisting end or state of affairs as its object, or entails a further reference to some nonexistent goal, he would claim that in some cases statements about conscious relations cannot be reduced to statements about physical relations. In such cases there would be a double incompleteness: one kind shared by physical relations, the other unique to conscious relations.

One point in Sartre's discussion of the connection between intentionality and purpose may cause some confusion for those familiar with Chisholm's work. Sartre emphasizes, as part of his concept of intentionality, that conscious relations may have nonexistent second terms. It was also pointed out that Chisholm has usually defended the somewhat different position, that an intentional statement does not imply "either that there is *or that there isn't* anything to which the expression truly applies" (italics mine).[27] This phrase suggests that Chisholm's use of the noninference criterion might prevent him from acknowledging Sartre's claim that we can speak of consciousness as intentional in cases where its object is definitely nonexistent. A reply to Chisholm can be found in Brentano himself.

Chisholm has discussed an early and a late position in Brentano's writings: the ontological thesis was first linked to, then dissociated from, the psychological thesis of intentionality. Chisholm points out that, in the second edition of *Psychologie vom empirischen Standpunkt*, Brentano thought psychical activity should be described as relational, rather than as containing its own objects. Brentano says that in physical relations both the Fundament and the Terminus of the relation have to exist. In the case of psychical relations, however, only the Fundament (i.e., the thinker) has to exist. Brentano points out that the object of thinking does not need to exist, and that in cases of a correct denial or rejection of something, the object of thought "must not exist."[28]

It should be emphasized that, in the passage just mentioned, Brentano proposed two somewhat different ways of making the distinction between mental and physical relations: the object of a psychical relation (a) need not exist and (b) must not exist. Chisholm has made the former move. It seems equally possible, however, to distinguish between mental and physical relations by using move (b). This is what Sartre does when he includes purpose (i.e., reference to nonexisting possibilities and goals) in the concept of intentionality. It may be that a full account of

27. Chisholm, "Brentano," pp. 21–22.
28. Ibid., p. 21. Chisholm cites Brentano, *Psychologie vom empirischen Standpunkt* (2d ed.; Leipzig, 1924), 2:133–34.

the "marks of intentionality" would require spelling out both moves.[29]

It should be added that Brentano qualified the term "relation" because of the peculiar nature of the Terminus; he suggested that what we are dealing with is something *like* a relation. Sartre needs to make a similar qualification A strong and a weak sense of the term "relation" (comparable to the earlier distinction between a strong and a weak sense of "reference") can be distinguished. Thus Sartre would claim that conscious relations—and *only* conscious relations—can be weak in the sense that they may have a nonexistent second term.

But why, under these circumstances, insist that consciousness is a relation of any kind, rather than, say, simply a property of the person? Sartre would remind us that all consciousness has the structure of being incomplete with respect to some specifiable object or state of affairs. It was pointed out earlier that it shares this characteristic with physical relations. Consciousness, for Sartre, is an internal relation, not in the sense that consciousness makes some difference to its object but in the sense that the object essentially characterizes the particular act of consciousness (*BN*, 86, 117). It can do so in at least two different ways. Sartre claims that we never simply think, we always think *of* something, whether it be an apple tree or a mathematical formula or a unicorn. Even where the object does not exist, the object serves to differentiate the separate thinkings.

In addition, the object can be used to distinguish different types of act, in the following way. My consciousness of an apple tree is either a perceiving or an imagining consciousness, depending on whether or not an apple tree is present.[30]

Many contemporary philosophers, confronted with Sartre's claim that some objects of consciousness are nonexistent, would use this as a conclusive reason for denying that consciousness is a relation of any sort.[31] John N. Deely has argued that this contemporary trend is an error, however, and that the classical view, going back to Aristotle, states that the relation derives its reality from its source in the subject, rather than from that

29. Both moves are subject to the difficulty that a traditional logic of dyadic relations requires that the second term of the relation must exist if valid inferences are to be made. It is possible to interpret Sartre as suggesting the need for a special logic of consciousness, here as at other points. However, it is an oversimplification of his position to say that he thinks consciousness is a dyadic relation. This point will be clarified shortly.

30. *Psychology of the Imagination*, p. 179.

31. E.g., Kenny, *Action, Emotion and Will*, p. 155. Also D. M. Armstrong,

which is referred to. Deely adds that the classical definition of a relation is "that modification or kind of being whose whole existence consists in reference to another."[32] Sartre's position seems quite similar to the classical when he says that consciousness "exhausts itself" in making a reference to its object (*BN*, li). Sartre's claim that consciousness is a kind of relation is controversial, then, to be sure; but given the classical tradition, it can hardly be treated as a meaningless position.[33]

Another point needs to be clarified. "Acts of consciousness" are not the only acts which are intentional in the double sense of referring purposively. For Sartre, human actions are conscious and are intentional in the same senses. He says "action necessarily implies as its condition the recognition of a 'desideratum'; that is, of an objective lack" (*BN*, 433). Elsewhere he clarifies the point that action deals with existing things, but does so in the light of what does not exist: "action, whatever it be, modifies that which is in the name of that which is not yet."[34]

In one of his articles Chisholm points out that doing as a causal modality is not intentional; however, trying and purposing are intentional. Since doing implies or involves one or another intentional attitude, Chisholm thinks that it is plausible to speak of acting as intentional.[35] This position can be contrasted with an earlier stand taken by Chisholm, when he discussed an example of Wittgenstein's: "I can look for him

---

A Materialist Theory of the Mind (London: Routledge & Kegan Paul; New York: Humanities Press, 1968), p. 40. It may be worth mentioning that Armstrong, who defends a central state theory, has to refer to the fact that there either is ,or is not an *external* stimulus in order to distinguish between perceiving and imagining (p. 300).

32. John N. Deely, "The Ontological Status of Intentionality." *New Scholasticism*, 46, no. 2 (Spring 1972): 225. Aristotle includes perception, knowledge, and attitudes among relations, and adds "the significance of all these is explained by a reference to something else and in no other way" (*Categories*, $7.6^b 2-4$).

33. There is still another way, however, that Sartre's claim that consciousness is a relation might be in error. Anthony Kenny has given a lucid account of some reasons why acts are sometimes confused with relations, and reasons why they should not be (*Action, Emotion and Will*, ch. 7). Sartre sometimes uses act or event terminology when speaking of consciousness, which suggests that he does not distinguish sharply between acts and relations (e.g., *BN*, pp. 74, 79). Since Sartre typically speaks of the for-itself as a relation, however, the distinction between strong and weak relations has been introduced to indicate what is peculiar to his view of conscious relations.

34. Jean-Paul Sartre, *Saint Genet: Actor and Martyr*, trans. Bernard Frechtman (New York: New American Library, 1963), p. 33.

35. Chisholm, "Some Psychological Concepts," p. 33.

when he is not there, but not hang him when he is not there."
Chisholm says that the first of these activities is intentional,
since it may be the case that its object does not exist. The
second, however, requires the existence and presence of the
object, and Chisholm says that it is "merely physical," presumably *because* the object exists.[36]

Sartre could claim, however, that it is a mistake to say that
the second activity is "merely physical." It is true that the man
who is hanged does actually exist. It is also the case that Sartre's
distinction between conscious relations and physical relations
makes use of the fact that the second term of a physical relation
must exist, while a conscious relation can have a nonexistent
object term.

If, however, what is meant by "hang" is that the agent has
some point in tying the rope around the man's neck—namely,
that he intends to bring about a not-yet-existing state of affairs
in which the now-living man is dead—then the action is intentional. The existing man, in other words, is not the *only* object
in this case; implicit reference is made to a further, nonexistent
object: the state of affairs the act is intended to bring about.

One could, of course, speak of "merely physical" activity if
the hanging resulted from a purely accidental human motion; or
a man might be hanged by a branch if he walked into a dark
thicket. But Sartre would describe conscious human action as
intentional, even if it were concerned with an existing object,
since a full description of that action would entail reference to a
not-yet-existing state of affairs (*BN*, 433).

At certain points Chisholm also wishes to speak of intentional attitudes even when the object of such an attitude exists.
His discussions of intentionality, using the noninference criterion, are most obviously applicable to such mental phenomena
as believing and thinking. However, he at times explicitly includes perceiving, knowing, and seeing among intentional psychological attitudes.[37] Since it is customary to analyze the
latter terms in a strong sense, as implying the existence of the
object perceived, known, or seen, they do not appear to meet
Chisholm's noninference criterion for intentional terms.

Chisholm's answer to this difficulty is given in an analysis of
the locution "there is something that S perceives to be f." This
entails the existence of f, but it also entails, among other

36. Roderick Chisholm, "Sentences about Believing," *Minnesota Studies*, 2:510. The Wittgenstein example is from *Philosophical Investigations*
(London and New York: Macmillan, 1953), p. 133e.
37. Chisholm, "Sentences about Believing," p. 511.

statements, that "*S takes* something to be *f*."[38] And sentences about taking something to be something meet Chisholm's non-inference criterion: to take or assume that the rocks are the reef does not imply either that the rocks are or are not the reef.[39] The fact that an existent object can be one of the objects of an act, then, is not sufficient reason—for either Chisholm or Sartre—to deny that the act is intentional, although Chisholm appears to take the opposing view in the hanging example.

For Sartre, the hanging example would show very clearly how human actions, as well as so-called "acts of consciousness," can be intentional: both can exhibit purposive reference. The existing man who is hanged is an added complication (speaking intentionally here, not morally). This action might be described as "*A* hanged *B* in order to *y*," where *B* is an existing object and *y* is an end or not-yet-existing state of affairs. But both reference and purpose are exhibited in "*A* hunted for *C* in order to *y*," where *C* might or might not exist, and in "*A* thought of *y*," and in "*A* saw *B* in the light of *y*." These also would count as intentional, in Sartre's view of intentionality.[40]

The question now needs to be asked whether the second version of Sartre's attack on the reducibility thesis is successful. Can a distinction be made between mental and physical relations on the basis that the second term of a mental relation can be nonexistent, while the second term of a physical relation must exist?

A direct challenge to the truth of this type of claim has been made in an article by Margaret A. Boden, in which she discusses Chisholm's views of intentionality. If it is recalled that Sartre says that human actions can exhibit intentionality, one of the cases she discusses appears to provide a good counterexample to Sartre's contention that physical relations must have existent second terms. Miss Boden suggests that a robot that has been

38. Chisholm, *Perceiving*, p. 168.
39. Ibid., p. 172. Cf. Sartre, *Psychology of Imagination*, p. 16.
40. The fact that Sartre treats consciousness as a relation, and the fact that there can be an existing object in addition to a nonexisting end, raise a question about just what kind of relation consciousness is supposed to be. For instance, some of these cases appear to be dyadic relations while others appear to be triadic. Moreover, the cases just mentioned do not exhaust the possibilities, as will be seen in the discussion of remembering.

This complexity does not seem to be an objection to Sartre's claim that an act of consciousness is a kind of (weak) relation; rather, it suggests that there may be as many kinds of conscious relations as there are physical relations. The fact of this complexity, however, reinforces the suggestion made earlier: Sartre's position points strongly to the need for a special logic of consciousness. In this case, a special logic would have to account for the variety of relations describable as conscious.

built to retrieve library books might be instructed to search for a nonexistent book. One could describe the rules which govern its search, including the criteria it uses for rejecting the books it finds, and one might program the robot with subroutines which permit it to stop when it acknowledges failure or to come up with some kind of substitute book.[41] Her example seems to provide good reason for rejecting or modifying Sartre's claims that only conscious existents can refer purposively, and that all physical relations must have an existent second term.

A somewhat different objection can also be made. If it were granted that purposive reference could serve as a way of distinguishing conscious relations from purely physical relations, could a distinction be made on the same basis between animal consciousness and human consciousness? The question must be taken seriously, I think, since one of Sartre's chief aims in developing the concept of intentionality is to support the claim that persons are moral agents. Chisholm has commented that he is not sure whether it is an advantage or a disadvantage that animals can be described, on a certain theory, as not possessing intentional attitudes.[42] Sartre, curiously enough, does not discuss the question. It was mentioned earlier that he distinguishes two basic forms of existence: things and consciousness. His discussions of consciousness frequently include the expression "human-reality" (e.g., BN, 95, 171). There seems to be little question that his discussion of the structures of the for-itself is intended to apply to human consciousness. It is simply unclear whether he would deny that animals are conscious, thereby classifying them as things, or, if he admitted that animals are conscious, whether he would claim they have consciousness of a different sort. Sartre's ontological world simply does not appear to include animals.

It would seem, however, that the basic points thus far made about the intentional structure of human consciousness would apply equally well to animal consciousness. Animals appear to be conscious of objects, and they seem to exhibit something very much like purpose. For instance, there seems to be something like reference to a nonexisting state of affairs, or reference to a future end, in the nesting behavior of birds.

It should be apparent that if Sartre's concept of intentionality includes no more than what has been discussed, then both of these examples—the book-seeking robot and the nest-building

41. Margaret A. Boden, "Intentionality and Physical Systems," *Philosophy of Science*, 37, no. 2 (June 1970): 212.
42. Chisholm, "Sentences about Believing," p. 515.

bird—can be used against Sartre's claim that nonconscious (and presumably nonhuman) things lack intentionality. Thus far it has been shown that when Sartre calls human consciousness intentional, he means that consciousness is a "lack" in relation to its object, and also that consciousness may have a nonexistent state of affairs as its object.

In criticism of Sartre's position it has been pointed out that physical relations may also be described as "lacking" their second terms, and that physical mechanisms and organisms, such as robots and animals, may be described as taking a nonexistent state of affairs as their object. Since Sartre's concept of intentionality is central to his attack on the reducibility thesis, Sartre must either admit that the reducibility thesis remains untouched or he must introduce some claims, in addition to the claim that consciousness is intentional in the senses already discussed, to complete his attack on the reducibility thesis. It is clear that Sartre has more to say on reducibility, but before we proceed in that direction it may be helpful to take special note of the "nothingness" terminology that surfaces repeatedly in his discussion of intentionality.

In particular, the interpretation developed thus far can be taken as a reply to a criticism of Sartre by A. J. Ayer and repeated by any English-speaking critics of Sartre. Sartre's use of "nothing" to mean consciousness has elicited great heat and caused considerable confusion. He has been accused of pessimism, trickery, and nonsense. Ayer compared Sartre's use of the expression *"le néant"* to the scene in which Alice, in her looking-glass adventure, claims to see nobody on the road, and the King replies that he wishes his eyes were good enough to be able to see Nobody too. Ayer continued by suggesting that Sartre used *"néant"* to name "something insubstantial and mysterious."[43] The criticism that Sartre misused the term "nothing" as a substantive would be very serious if it were correct; and it has been repeated by other critics of Sartre.[44]

In answer to the critics, it can be admitted that Sartre's choice of terms has caused confusion, but it can be pointed out that if Sartre meant to startle a particular fly out of the

43. A. J. Ayer, "Novelist-Philosophers: V. Jean-Paul Sartre," *Horizon*, 12 (July 1945):18, 19.
44. E.g., Van Meter Ames, "Fetichism in the Existentialism of Sartre," *Journal of Philosophy*, 47 (July 6, 1950): 408–11. Also Wilfred Desan, *The Tragic Finale: An Essay on the Philosophy of Jean-Paul Sartre* (rev. ed.; New York: Harper & Row, 1960), pp. 140–41.

philosophical flybottle—namely, the common assumption that mind or consciousness is a self-subsisting container filled with sense data or intentional objects—his choice of terms is not without point.

Ayer's criticism overlooks the fact that, far from using it to refer to an "insubstantial and mysterious" substance, Sartre used the term "nothing" (or "*néant*") in part to *deny* that consciousness is a thing or substance.[45] He used it in part to affirm that an act of consciousness is a relation, that is, a "lack" or incompleteness requiring an object; and he used it in part as a way of suggesting that conscious relations, unlike physical ones, could have nonexistent objects.[46]

There has been another confusion concerning Sartre's use of "*néant*" to mean consciousness. Sartre does not mean, as Wilfred Desan thinks he means, that consciousness does not exist.[47] Sartre says "there are only two types of existence, as thing in the world and as consciousness."[48]

Sartre's terminology should not be wholly unfamiliar to the English-speaking reader, however. What he says about consciousness as nothingness can be compared, for instance, with the passage in which G. E. Moore describes an attempt to focus attention on consciousness, only to discover that it disappears. Only the blue remains when we try to discover the blue sensation; the rest, says Moore, is "mere emptiness."[49] William James, discussing this passage of Moore's, agreed that consciousness is here in danger of evaporating completely; consciousness becomes a "nonentity." James added the emphatic point, later in this article, that while consciousness is not an entity, it is a relation.[50] Sartre's terminology is sufficiently similar to that of

45. Etymological support can be given here for Sartre. The French masculine noun *néant* is derived from the Latin *nec entem*, meaning *pas un être*, not a being (*Larousse classique dictionnaire encyclopédique* [Paris: Librairie Larousse, 1957], p. 792).

46. For another discussion of Sartre's use of "nothing" see Arne Naess, *Four Modern Philosophers: Carnap, Wittgenstein, Heidegger, Sartre*, trans. Alastair Hannay (Chicago and London: University of Chicago Press, 1968), pp. 295–308. Also Alvin C. Plantinga, "An Existentialist's Ethics," *Review of Metaphysics*, 12 (December 1958): 236–39, 251–55.

47. Desan, *The Tragic Finale*, p. 141.

48. Jean-Paul Sartre, *Imagination: A Psychological Critique*, trans. Forrest Williams (Ann Arbor: University of Michigan Press, 1962), p. 116.

49. Moore, "The Refutation of Idealism," p. 25.

50. William James, "Does 'Consciousness' Exist?" in *Essays in Radical Empiricism and a Pluralistic Universe* (New York: Longmans, Green, 1943), pp. 2–3, 25.

Moore and James that his use of *"néant"* might have caused less confusion.[51]

If the present interpretation is correct, neither of the frequently quoted criticisms of Sartre's use of "nothingness" terminology is sound; it is not the case that he misuses *"néant"* as a substantive, nor does he use the term to support the claim that consciousness itself does not exist. On the other hand, Sartre can certainly be criticized, in another way, for his use of this type of expression. The real problem is that Sartre's peculiar "nothingness" terminology represents the following misleading claims.

In using *"néant"* to mean consciousness, and in spelling out the claim that consciousness alone is intentional, it was found that Sartre means that consciousness is a "lack" in relation to an object, and that that object may be a nonexisting state of affairs. But he clearly means to contrast consciousness to nonconscious things (and probably to animal consciousness). His "nothingness" terminology, as thus far discussed, fails to suggest a genuine distinction if it is true that a physical relation as well as a conscious relation can "lack" its second term, and if it is true that a physical mechanism or an animal organism can have a nonexistent end.

There is, however, an additional claim within the concept of intentionality, which may, I think, suggest the genuine distinction Sartre is seeking. The idea of intentionality includes still another form of nothingness, and it is to this that we must now turn.

The Third Argument Against Reducibility:
Intentionality as Chosen Purpose

Sartre's third argument against the reducibility thesis is implicit in his famous doctrine that in human beings alone does existence precede essence. This doctrine and its clarification will

---

51. Cf. John Passmore, *A Hundred Years of Philosophy* (rev. ed.; New York: Basic Books, 1966), pp. 508–9. Passmore notes the similarity in terminology between Sartre and Moore and James; he does not, however, emphasize the conceptual point of similarity which underlies the terminological similarity: for all three, consciousness is a relation (cf. supra, n. 15).

provide one of the major themes throughout the remainder of this book, and it can be sketched as follows.

The "ends" of animals are relatively fixed and common to other members of the species. The instructions about what the robot will seek, and how it will go about that search, are programmed into the mechanism. One may wish to speak of animals and robots as having purposes (although Sartre does not do so), but only human consciousness can imagine possible alternative purposes and can choose among them. In human beings there are no ultimate (nonbiological) ends common to all men, and this is a fact of central importance for man as a moral agent. Each man chooses his own ends, and can adopt new ones, even ends diametrically opposed to those held earlier (*BN*, 407, 564, 566–68).[52]

For Sartre, the ability to imagine and to choose from a variety of ends depends in part on the distinctively human capacity for reflection, that is, the ability to take one's own intending as the object of further intentions (*BN*, 440). The ability to reflect is not easy to account for, and will be discussed in later chapters, as will Sartre's concept of choice.

In the concept of intentionality, then, there are three major forms of "nothingness": (1) the conscious relation (as any other type of relation) is a "lack" in the sense that it requires a second term; (2) the conscious relation can have a nonexistent end as its second term; and (3) there is no particular predetermined end or purpose for persons, as there is in the case of machines and animals.

Of these three claims based on forms of "nothingness," only the third has turned out to be unique to human conscious relations. Does this mean that Sartre's attack on the reducibility thesis is substantially weakened? Certainly it is not as convincing as Sartre might have liked. At least one reply that he might make, however, would be that the one remaining distinction is sufficient to establish his claim that statements about (human) mental phenomena cannot be reduced to statements about wholly physical phenomena.

A more extended reply, however, can be developed by asking what further conclusion, if any, is supposed to follow from

52. Sartre is not denying that all men need to eat, have sex, etc. But *how* we eat, form sexual attachments, etc., depends on individually chosen ends (cf. *BN*, p. 407). More central to the idea of the person as a moral agent, however, is the fact that human purposes range far beyond the limits of organic survival.

Sartre's attack on the reducibility thesis. Chisholm, for instance, in arguing for the intentionality of mental phenomena, has maintained that "if this view is true, then the basic thesis of physicalism and the unity of science is false."[53] But Sartre did not move from the claim that the reducibility thesis is false to the broader claim that physicalism is false. In *Being and Nothingness* Sartre said that his project was to describe conscious phenomena, not to explain them (p. 620). He tried to show that there is no "insurmountable dualism" between things and consciousness. What he meant by this is that since consciousness *is* a relation to objects, there is no problem of showing any further connection. There is not the kind of difficulty Descartes faced in saying there are physical substances and mental substances, and then having to show how these totally unlike realms of being could have any connection with each other, since for Sartre consciousness exists originally *as* a relation to things.

This does not mean, however, that Sartre claimed to defend one of the traditional monistic positions. In an article written a few years after the publication of *Being and Nothingness*, Sartre attacked both materialism and idealism as forms of reductionist metaphysics. He added that experience shows only that there is some kind of firm connection between psychological and physical phenomena, without giving decisive evidence in favor of any particular metaphysical interpretation of that link.[54]

Sartre objected to the reductionism of both materialism and idealism. Nor did he intend to espouse an "insurmountable dualism." Should his position therefore be described as a "surmountable" dualism? If so, it appears at first glance to be a dualism of a very strange kind, for it divides reality not into two kinds of substance but into substances or physical objects, on the one hand, and into one kind of relation, consciousness, on the other hand. What is central to the notion of consciousness is intentionality, in the sense of selective, purposive reference.

It can be noted that in her article on robots and intentionality, Miss Boden was quite willing to admit that certain forms of behavior are intentional, but she objected to the specific claim that these forms of behavior could not be explained in physical terms.[55] Sartre's terminology suggests that he intended to make

53. Chisholm, "Intentionality," p. 203.
54. Jean-Paul Sartre, "Materialism and Revolution," in *Jean-Paul Sartre: Literary and Philosophical Essays*, trans. Annette Michelson (New York: Collier Books, 1962), pp. 200–201. This essay first appeared in the June/July 1946 issue of *Les Temps Modernes*.
55. Boden, "Intentionality and Physical Systems," p. 200.

a radical distinction between physical things and consciousness. One of the points that has become clear in the preceding discussion, however, is that the actual claims underlying his terminology do not commit him to a two-substance dualism. Since Sartre has definitely avoided committing himself to the position that physicalism is false, one might reinterpret his terminology as representing logical, not ontological, distinctions. It is possible that Sartre might even be able to accept a form of physicalism which is complex enough to incorporate the irreducibly intentional features of consciousness within its explanatory framework.[56]

There is, however, at least one other possibility. Sartre's position might still be described as a two-substance view, depending on the nature of the individual who is conscious. That is, Sartre's discussion of the referentiality of consciousness, and of the difficulties to be found in the view that intentional objects are immanent in consciousness, provides reasons for saying that consciousness is a relation, rather than a substance. But the *subject* term of that relation might still be a non-physical substance, that is, an immaterial person or ego, even if consciousness is not a substance. One of Sartre's critics, in fact, claims that Sartre must be committed to just such a position. This possibility is one that will be discussed in the next chapter.

If Sartre is able to give satisfactory reasons for believing there are no immaterial person-substances, his open reluctance to commit himself to an explanation of the irreducibility that he has described will have to be taken seriously. In attacking the view that descriptions of conscious relations can be reduced to descriptions of physical phenomena or relations, Sartre has emphasized a distinction central to the concept of the person as a moral agent, as we will see. This, rather than whether a particular explanatory metaphysic is implied by his attack on the reducibility thesis, appears to be the important point underlying his discussion of intentionality.

56. Sartre may in fact have moved closer to such a position in his more recent work, which represents an existentialist variation of dialectical materialism. Hazel Barnes has described some of the new developments in Sartre's thinking about man's relations to the physical world in her illuminating essay introducing Sartre's *Search for a Method* (New York: Vintage Books, 1963), pp. vii–xxxi. This work is a translation of the preface to volume 1 of Sartre's long philosophical work, *Critique de la Raison Dialectique*, published in 1960; most of the *Critique* is not yet available in translation.

Chapter 2

The Question of Separate Existence

Included in the controversy whether there is a logical connection between persons and their bodies is the question whether statements about psychological phenomena can be reduced without remainder to statements about physical phenomena. It has been argued that Sartre's discussion would permit him to distinguish between intentional and nonintentional phenomena, but that this distinction may not enable him to deny that statements about the psychological could be reduced to statements about the physical.

Another issue within the general question whether there is a logical connection between persons and their bodies is that of separate existence. This can be subdivided into the questions (a) whether it is logically possible that minds (selves, persons, experiences, etc.) could exist separately from bodies in general, as in the case of life after death, or (b) whether it is logically possible that minds (persons, experiences, etc.) could exist apart from the original body in particular, as in the case of a person changing to another body.[1] Some moral implications of the change-of-body thesis will be discussed.

These issues can be raised apropos of Sartre's claim that consciousness is not a substance and, furthermore, that it is a relation. His position has led Wilfred Desan to argue that in making consciousness a relation, Sartre unwittingly presupposed the existence of an immaterial ego as the subject term of conscious relations.[2] Such an ego might exist separately from all bodies, or from the original body. Sartre claims, however, that the human body is the subject term of conscious relations (*BN*, 305, 316). This claim will be discussed and clarified. Sartre

---

1. These must be considered as distinct questions—by P. F. Strawson, for instance, who thinks it is necessarily the case that a person has material characteristics, but does not deny that two persons could alternately share the same body or that one person could conceivably switch bodies. See his *Individuals: An Essay in Descriptive Metaphysics* (Garden City, N.Y.: Doubleday, 1959), pp. 113, 114, 131–32.
2. Desan, *The Tragic Finale*, pp. 151–52.

claims, also, that it is unnecessary to posit the existence of an additional immaterial subject.[3] It will be shown how Sartre's claim that the body is the subject of acts of consciousness can be used in reply to Desan's arguments.

First, what can Sartre mean by saying that the human body is the subject term of conscious relations? In the first place, he is not making the claim that we *experience* the body *qua* subject; to the contrary, he notes that the eye does not see itself seeing (*BN*, 304, 316). What Sartre is doing can be clarified by recalling that in 1914 Bertrand Russell held the position that experiencing is a relation, one term of which is the experienced object and the other term is the experiencer. The strongest objection to this analysis, Russell claimed, is that we are unable to introspect the subject. He proposed two ways of meeting the objection: (a) maintain that we are acquainted with the subject or (b) maintain that even if the theory is true, there is no reason why we should have acquaintance with the subject.[4] Sartre makes the latter move.

To say that the body is the subject of conscious acts, and to say also that we do not experience the body as the subject of conscious acts, is to claim that the body is only implicit in an analysis of our own conscious experience. This point is connected with Sartre's important distinction between reflective and unreflective levels of consciousness. It can be clarified by some of Sydney Shoemaker's diagrams and some diagrams suggested by those of Shoemaker.

In our ordinary, unreflective relations with the world, says Sartre, the body is the center from which we intend objects, but it is not usually an additional object of experience. Our direct, unreflective consciousness of objects should be described, he says, as " 'pre-personal,' *without an I*" (*TE*, 36). That is to say, we are usually directly aware of an object, but not explicitly of ourselves being aware of (desiring, thinking of, etc.) that object. Shoemaker tries to represent this simple fact of our experience (with respect to several objects of awareness) in Diagram A.[5]

3. Jean-Paul Sartre, *The Transcendence of the Ego: An Existentialist Theory of Consciousness*, trans. Forrest Williams and Robert Kirkpatrick (New York: Noonday Press, 1957), p. 40. Subsequent references to this work will be abbreviated *TE* and noted parenthetically in the text.

4. Bertrand Russell, "On the Nature of Acquaintance," in *Logic and Knowledge: Essays*, ed. Robert Charles Marsh (New York: Macmillan, 1956), pp. 162–63.

5. Reprinted from Sydney Shoemaker, *Self-Knowledge and Self-Identity* (Ithaca, N.Y.: Cornell University Press, 1963), p. 70. © 1963 by Cornell University. Used by permission of Cornell University Press.

Diagram A   (Shoemaker)

$$O^1$$

$$O^2$$

$$O^3$$

Sartre, however, would object to this as a representation of the fact that we are aware of objects directly, because the objects are not shown as perceived from any particular angle. Sartre has attacked the position, which appears to be represented in Shoemaker's diagram, that assumes we might perceive objects "objectively," that is, from all sides at once (*BN*, 306–7).

A better diagram for representing Sartre's claim that we are directly aware of an object, but that we are aware of it from a particular vantage point, would be Diagram B.

Diagram B

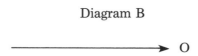 O

One has to imagine that one is standing at the place indicated by the nonpointed end of the arrow, but one's own body is not an additional object of perception. It is, rather, the central point from which perception takes place, and it is the continuing point of reference. This, most simply, is what Sartre means by saying that the body is the subject of conscious relations to objects, but that the body is not ordinarily an additional object of experience. It should be noted that the diagram does *not* represent the vantage point of the outsider, who could, of course, observe both terms of the perceptual relation represented. Rather, it represents the experience of an object from the vantage point of the experiencer (body-subject), who *is* the first term in the relation.

As indicated in Diagram B, the structure of unreflective consciousness is "pre-personal." That is, it is directed upon the object of awareness and not upon myself being aware of an object. "There was no *I* in the unreflected consciousness," says Sartre, speaking of our experience, and not of the total situation (*TE*, 47). It is for this reason that Sartre thinks the basic form of perceptual statement is "there is consciousness of this chair" (*TE*, 53–54).[6] Shoemaker, making a point similar to Sartre's, says that while we perceive only "*objects* of perception (a tautology)," philosophers have thought of this situation as if we perceive *ourselves* perceiving objects. Shoemaker represents this traditional philosophical belief in Diagram C.[7]

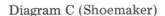

Diagram C (Shoemaker)

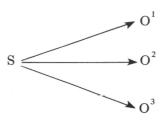

But no one actually perceives this, Shoemaker adds; it is only our thinking of it in this way that suggests that the subject should be perceivable.

Sartre would agree that Diagram C is a misrepresentation of what we experience on the unreflective level of awareness. But Diagram C might represent the relation between a body-subject and several objects of perception, as viewed by an *outside* observer. Furthermore, Sartre can account for the prevalence of this philosophical confusion by noting that the same diagram comes close to representing what we encounter as an *object* in acts of reflection.

The structure of reflective experience can be represented by Diagram D, which is suggested by Shoemaker's diagrams. It should be noted that this diagram again takes the vantage point of the experiencer, and not an outside stance. The single prereflective act that is the object of reflection occurs at a particular

6. Cf. Bertrand Russell, *The Analysis of Mind* (London: Allen & Unwin, 1921; New York: Macmillan, 1921), p. 18. Russell here prefers the impersonal " 'it thinks in me' " since " 'I think so-and-so' " "suggests that thinking is the act of a person."

7. Shoemaker, *Self-Knowledge and Self-Identity*, p. 67. © 1963 by Cornell University. Used by permission of Cornell University Press. Quotation from p. 73.

time, t_1, while the reflective act occurs later, at t_2. For simplicity, the prereflective act is represented as directed toward a single object, instead of three simultaneous objects.

Diagram D

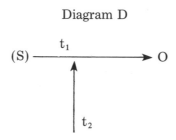

I, the body-subject, perform this reflective act; since I do not directly experience my own brain, I place myself in the empty space at the nonpointed end of the vertical arrow. (If I were representing the fact, rather than *my experience* of the fact, the body-subject would be shown instead of that space at the lower end of the vertical arrow.) The vertical arrow represents the reflective act which takes, as object, the prior act performed by the body-subject. Since it *is* experienced as part of the object for reflection, and not as a subject, the S which represents the body-subject in Diagram D is enclosed in parentheses.

The interesting point, for Sartre, is that in reflection I take something like an outsider's position with respect to the earlier act performed by me. It is this move to an objective stance with respect to my conscious acts which makes me aware of the body-subject, even though it is a retrospective awareness. Thus it is in reflection upon a prior intention that the ego or "I" first appears in our experience (*TE*, 53, 83).[8]

To say "*I have* consciousness of this chair," then, is to make a reflective judgment on a prior act of direct, unreflective awareness of the chair by the body-subject.[9]

Sartre puts this point slightly differently when he says that "the ego is not the owner of consciousness; it is the object of

8. Cf. Russell, "On the Nature of Acquaintance," pp. 162, 167. Russell distinguishes between experiencing O and experiencing our own experiencing of O; we can know O without reflecting on our experiencing of O. This is comparable to Sartre's distinction between reflective and unreflective levels of consciousness.

9. Cf. Gilbert Ryle, *The Concept of Mind* (New York: Barnes & Noble, 1949), pp. 195–98. Ryle's account of the "systematic elusiveness of 'I' " is based on the retrospective nature of "higher order actions." Cf. Sartre, *TE*, p. 88: the ego never appears, says Sartre, "except 'out of the corner of the eye.' "

consciousness" (*TE*, 97). The ego, furthermore, is not the object of a single reflective awareness but is a synthetic "ideal object." That is, Sartre says the reflective use of "I" simply connects the act reflected upon to previous acts and states of the body-subject (*TE*, 91, 100).[10] A more complete discussion of the nature of this ideal object will be given later. The point, however, is to show that, for Sartre, the body is not ordinarily directly experienced as a subject but is experienced only retrospectively as an object, and an object not of perception but reflection.

Sartre claims that there is a very good reason to think we cannot experience the subject *qua* subject directly. The reason is that if the subject were a direct object of experience, another subject would have to be the subject of experiencing the subject, and this would lead to an infinite regress.

Thus if Diagram C were taken to represent what I actually experience at a particular time, t_1, and not simply an outsider's view of my relation to objects, it would have to be supposed that there is an additional subject at t_1 who experiences S-perceiving-an-object at t_1. Sartre says there would then be at least two *I*'s, one of reflected consciousness, the other of the reflecting consciousness. One of Husserl's disciples, Fink, had even picked out a third *I* (*TE*, 52). There is no need, however, to experience a subject in order to be directly aware of objects, although there must of course *be* a subject of awareness. Thus a description of my unreflective conscious experience has no need of an *I* (*TE*, 53).[11]

It can be noted that there is no infinite regress in reflective experience, however, since Sartre's account of this requires only that the same subject who performed an unreflective act of awareness at t_1 now, at t_2, reflects on this earlier act.

This is Sartre's argument in support of the claim that while there must be a subject of unreflective consciousness, it is not and cannot be directly experienced *qua* subject. It was pointed out earlier that Russell had maintained that one of the strongest objections to an analysis of experience into a relation between a subject and an object is that we are not directly acquainted with

10. Cf. Russell, *Analysis of Mind*, p. 18: "the person is not an ingredient in the single thought: he is rather constituted by relations of the thoughts to each other and to the body."

11. Cf. Russell, "On the Nature of Acquaintance," p. 167. Russell also points out that there is no need to experience our experiencing in order to experience objects; there would be an infinite regress if it were otherwise, he said.

a subject. And Russell suggested that one way of meeting this objection was to argue that there is no reason why we should have acquaintance with a subject. Sartre's distinction between reflective and unreflective levels of consciousness, and his argument that an infinite regress would occur if we thought of ourselves as directly, rather than reflectively, acquainted with the subject, can be interpreted as Russell suggested.

Sartre's discussion thus far, however, will support only part of the point he wished to make. His point was not only that we do not directly experience the subject but also that the body is the subject of conscious relations. Russell said that since we do not have direct acquaintance with the subject, we cannot know whether it is physical or mental.[12] As we will see, Sartre's central argument for saying the subject term of conscious relations is the body is that there is no need to posit the existence of an extra entity, an immaterial person-substance, as the subject (*TE*, 40).

One reason why thinkers have believed there must be an immaterial subject in addition to the body has been that first-person psychological statements seem to make no reference to the body. Shoemaker, among others, discusses the statement "I have a toothache." One can know the truth of this statement without observing any body. Shoemaker points out that people have tended to conclude from this that the "I" must therefore refer to a person which is a nonbody.[13]

According to Sartre, one source of confusion in this type of reasoning is to think that one's own body must occupy the same role in one's experience as the bodies of others. In a long discussion of pain, he points out that one's own pain can either be lived (sometimes he says "existed") or it can be made the object of a special intention, that is, be treated reflexively. If we live our pain, it simply becomes an element in our direct awareness of other objects: there is a painful seeing of a tree or a headachy thought of a triangle. But it is also possible to make an object of the pain itself, to experience the headache as the focus of awareness (*BN*, 305, 332–37).

Now of course one must observe the grimaces of others and their swollen jaws to find out if they have a toothache, and of course one does not have to look in a mirror to know if one has a toothache oneself. But the suggestion that what one knows about bodies can be known only in the way that one knows

12. Ibid., p. 164.
13. Shoemaker, *Self-Knowledge and Self-Identity*, pp. 16, 17.

about the bodies of others is wholly unwarranted, and there is no reason to deny that "I have a toothache" makes a reference to the body. The body as subject term of conscious relations can, on occasion, become reflexively aware of some of its own states and conditions. Some of these conditions are strictly "physical." For example, we can know, even when our feet are out of sight, which foot is crossed on top of the other foot. Thus, contrary to what many contemporary philosophers have thought, the fact that one knows differently from the way other people know what state one's own body is in is surely no guarantee of that state's being nonphysical. Nor can privileged access to certain kinds of information be used as a conclusive reason for the existence of an immaterial subject.

If the conscious subject of experience were a nonbodily person, something substantially different from the body itself, then Sartre could turn the tables and ask how it is that the nonbodily person knows of a toothache. Since it is alleged to be something other than the body, mustn't this person observe the grimaces and swollen jaw of its body, just as it would have to observe the facial expression and facial contour of others' bodies, if it is to learn of a toothache?

Furthermore, if "I have a toothache" does not make a reference to any body, where is the tooth that aches? If it is a mind's tooth, how could a physical dentist locate the cavity, say, and cure the toothache? In fact, however, Sartre would claim that "I have a toothache" does make a reference to one's body, a body which is a conscious subject and can become reflexively aware of some of its own states. Only if we assume that the body is insentient, that the body is a nonconscious habitation for another conscious subject, are we led to the strange suggestion that "I have a toothache" makes no reference to the body. Sartre says "being-for-itself must be wholly body and it must be wholly consciousness; it cannot be *united* with a body" (*BN*, 305).

It has been suggested that Sartre's account can readily handle the everyday cases, and can handle these more satisfactorily than if one were to add a nonbodily subject to the picture. There have been certain traditional problem cases, however, such as phantom limbs. Would Sartre have to give up a claim that "I have a toothache" is a form of reflexive reference to the body-subject if "I have a pain in my left foot" turns out to be false because the left foot has been amputated?

Sartre could explain this type of case, which would be a special case of the general problem of how we can make

erroneous judgments, in the following way. He has given reasons
for rejecting the apparatus of intentional objects within a correspondence theory of truth. One does not need to refer to
properties of intentional objects in order to explain erroneous
judgments. In fact, as he argued, intentional objects are superfluous in this role, since one could never make the judgment that
one's ideas were false unless one had access to the real objects.
There are at least two ways in which Sartre's theory can handle
the problem of error, and both would seem to be applicable to
the case of phantom limbs.

In the first place, one can account for perceptual errors by
examining the structure and condition of the visual equipment
itself; many perceptual mistakes can be explained by reference
to damaged optical nerves, changes in the curvature of the lens
of the eye, the effects of drugs on the nervous system, etc.
Merleau-Ponty has pointed out that the phantom limb experience disappears once the appropriate nerves leading to the brain
are cut.[14] Sartre clearly could use this point in defense of his
own position.

Sartre might supplement this explanation by recalling that
part of what is meant by saying that consciousness is an intentional relation is that reference can be made to objects or states
of affairs that do not exist. There seems to be no good reason
why that point cannot be extended to the case of phantom
limbs. Sartre definitely does not claim that our reflexive awareness is incorrigible; he distinguishes between an area of certainty
and a domain of doubtfulness in reflection (*TE*, 64). In the case
of the phantom limb, he could say there is a real experience of
pain but there is a false judgment concerning the location of the
pain. So far there seems to be no good reason to posit the
existence of an extra entity, a nonbodily person, to account for
phantom limbs.

A more extended account of why Sartre claims that "the
transcendental *I* . . . has no *raison d'être*" needs to be given (*TE*,
40). Sartre's reasons in support of this claim can be given most
conveniently in the form of answers to several arguments
against his position made by Wilfred Desan, and more recently
by John D. Scanlon. Desan maintains that Sartre, in making
consciousness a relation, has presupposed an ego or immaterial
person as the subject term of that relation. Desan's arguments,

14. M. Merleau-Ponty, *Phenomenology of Perception*, trans. Colin
Smith (London: Routledge & Kegan Paul, 1962; New York: Humanities
Press, 1962), p. 77.

while based on what seems to be a serious misunderstanding of Sartre's position, are interesting because they are the traditional arguments offered in favor of the claim that immaterial subjects must exist.

To begin, Desan says that in claiming the ego does not exist, Sartre has denied there is a "permanent and underlying entity" in human beings which would permit us to use the locutions "*I am* or *I think*."[15] But Desan begins with an error: Sartre does not deny such an entity in human beings. In Sartre's own words, "not that the psyche is *united* to a body but that . . . the body is its substance and its perpetual condition of possibility" (*BN*, 338). The point is that Sartre denies a two-substance view of persons, not a one-substance view, as Desan and Scanlon seem to think.

It was pointed out earlier that the body-subject is directly aware of objects, but that it can also reflect upon its previous acts of awareness. Sartre can account for both the "I am" and the "I think" by his claim that the body itself is the conscious subject of acts of awareness and that it can reflect upon these acts. The "I" of "I think" is not an extra entity but is rather the partial product of an extra act, the reflective act which takes a previous thinking as its object. The ideal object, "I," which is a synthetic connection of the act-reflected-upon with previous acts of the body-subject, has an existence also (*TE*. 52, 76). But the ego exists as a pattern of acts, not as a substance (*TE*, 92). Sartre frequently uses the analogy of a melody which exists as a coherent pattern of sounds that are struck, note by note. This synthetic object, the ego, will be discussed in detail in later chapters. For now, the point is only that it is not an extra entity or substance.

There is another argument against the impersonality of Sartre's view of the for-itself, which Desan calls an elaboration of the traditional argument against Hume's attack on the Self. The Self is required as "the center of my acts," since a relational analysis of the for-itself presupposes "a *terminus a quo* as well as a *terminus ad quem*." Desan adds that the *I* must be presupposed as the subject of acts such as knowing, desiring a glass of water, choosing, and negating.[16]

---

15. Desan, *The Tragic Finale*, p. 149. A similar objection is made in John D. Scanlon, "Consciousness, the Streetcar, and the Ego: *Pro* Husserl, *Contra* Sartre," *Philosophical Forum*, no. 2 (Spring 1971), p. 350. Scanlon assumes that any such underlying entity must be a transcendental ego.

16. Desan, *The Tragic Finale*, pp. 151–52.

Sartre can agree with several of Desan's points. It is true that I exist; it is true that I am the center of my acts; it is true that a relation requires a *terminus a quo* as well as a *terminus ad quem* (although the latter may be, for Sartre, an object or state of affairs that is nonexistent). But it does not follow from any of these points, or from all of them taken together, that the *I* is an immaterial person-substance or ego. Sartre says the body is the "center of action" (*BN*, 320).

Sartre's analysis of this point is similar to his analysis of the special place the body occupies in perception. The body is the continuing point of view *from which* other objects in the world are seen. The body is "that in relation to which the perceived object indicates its distance" (*BN*, 326).[17] In action, also, the body occupies a special position. For each of us, Sartre says, the "world" consists of an organization of objects into an "instrumental complex"; that is, the "world" is a way of grouping and classifying things with reference to our own purposes (*BN*, 322, 325). Within this instrumental complex, Sartre says, the human body occupies a special position. It is not itself an instrument to be used but is the "unutilizable instrument" indicated by all other object-instruments. It would be a mistake, that is, to think of the body as a tool to be used by a mind or a person. We see a hammer, and view it as an instrument with which to drive in the nail; but we do not in the same way view our hand as an instrument with which to lift the hammer (*BN*, 320–25).

In our basic unreflective relations with the world we see objects as things "to be lifted," "to be climbed over"; we see them, in other words, as describable within a framework which includes an implicit reference to the action this body might or will take toward those objects. The body as unutilizable, inapprehensible center of the instrumental complex of things is "a necessary condition of my action" (*BN*, 327). Is there need for *two* centers of actions? Desan has not shown this, nor does it seem to be a plausible requirement. Sartre asks, isn't this enough? "Need one double it with a transcendental *I*?" (*TE*, 36).

Sartre's answer to the next group of arguments offered by Desan is somewhat more complicated. Desan says that an ego is needed to provide a unifying connection among our experiences. He admits that Sartre has given a partly satisfactory

---

17. Cf. Hampshire's comment that reference is ultimately linked to the gesture of pointing, and that pointing is always done from a place to a place (*Thought and Action*, pp. 54, 55).

answer when Sartre says that external objects provide one way of specifying consciousness. But Desan claims there is also need of a permanent subject which is aware of objects, which can provide spatial as well as chronological unity for experience.[18]

The basic error in Desan's argument, here as before, is to ignore what Sartre has said about the conscious human body as the subject term of conscious relations. The body can provide a unified subject in single acts of awareness; it can provide both a spatial and a chronological unity. The body is in the spatial center of situations, and it persists as a subject from birth to death. This point does not seem to require elaboration. There are other ways in which Sartre accounts for unity, however, which need further discussion.

A second kind of unity important to Sartre's concept of a person can be mentioned. Sartre, as we have seen, claims that the human body is the subject term of the consciousness relation. Over a period of time, each individual develops a pattern or system of conscious relations to objects and to people—what is usually called character or personality, and what Sartre usually calls the ego. It will be shown later that this system is organized with reference to a fundamental project or ideal self, according to Sartre. The continuity of such a pattern of relations helps account for the fact that a situation makes sense. At times, a radically new pattern of relations to other people and to objects can develop. For Sartre, the sense of unity through time is in part a function of the persistence of the body-subject, but it also depends on the persistence of a certain basic pattern of acting and thinking (*TE*, 60, 76; *BN*, 561). This type of unity does not require any substance other than the body-subject itself.

Two other ways of accounting for unity can be discussed in more detail. Consciousness is not a private box, Sartre has argued, but rather a continuing relation that a particular body has with objects. Sartre has objected to (among other things) the spatial image underlying the container view of consciousness (*BN*, 314). Only things exist in space. On the other hand, "the for-itself cannot be except in temporal form" (*BN*, 136). Sartre means two things by this. First, acts of awareness are events; one can specify a time at which one is conscious of x. To be conscious of x, as in visual perception, is not to dislodge a facsimile of x—a sensation or intentional object—from the sur-

18. Desan, *The Tragic Finale*, pp. 152–53. Cf. Scanlon, "Consciousness," p. 350.

face of x, and then drop this into our private inner box. Rather, for Sartre, to intend x is to be present to x itself; presence to____defines the temporal present, Sartre says (*BN*, 121). [19] The use here of a spatial term, "presence," does not mean that consciousness itself is spatial but rather refers to the spatial *origin* of consciousness, the body-subject.

The act of awareness occurs at a given time. But acts of awareness are never limited to the present instant, says Sartre (*BN*, 142, 149). Each intention is structured as a temporal synthesis; this is the second claim Sartre makes concerning the temporality of consciousness. Perception, for instance, is always richer than what one sees. To see object x *as* object x is in part to re-cognize it; that is, to see it in comparison with past experiences of this and similar objects. In addition, to see object x as object x is in part to expect it to figure in future perceptions and experiences in certain predictable ways, and to view it as connected with some future end. [20] This unification of past and future in each present act of awareness helps account for the sense of chronological unity, and also contributes to the fact that a given situation makes sense. If there were no temporal synthesis such as Sartre describes, each seeing would be utterly new and disconnected from every other; each moment would bring a fresh chaos.

A correlative aspect of the sense of personal identity through time is the persistence of objects. It would be impossible to account for the kind of temporal synthesis of consciousness just described if it were not for the fact that many objects of consciousness are met with repeatedly, and kinds of objects are encountered again and again. There is a frequent sense of disorientation or strangeness when one wakes up in a strange city or enters a new group. If there were no continuity of objects of consciousness, there might be a permanent sense of disorientation. If, on the other hand, objects are withdrawn completely, there is a disintegration of ego functioning in general, and of the ability to think and to concentrate in particular,

19. Cf. Russell, "On the Nature of Acquaintance," p. 168: "the time of the things which have to 'I' the relation of presence is called the present time."

20. Sartre, *Psychology of the Imagination*, pp. 172–73. Cf. Scanlon ("Consciousness," p. 337), who argues that the fact of self-unification can only be accounted for by positing an ego. For a very different interpretation of Sartre's idea of time, which places primary emphasis on the present instant, see Marjorie Grene, *Sartre* (New York: New Viewpoints, 1973), p. 64.

as recent experiments have shown.[21] Sartre mentions different examples of continuing objects which contribute to the sense of personal unity through time; among them are physical objects and mathematical truths (*TE*, 38, 49).

Desan has claimed that Sartre cannot account for the sense of personal unity without presupposing a persisting ego. In answer to Desan, it can be said that an immaterial subject appears to be neither a necessary nor a sufficient condition of being aware of oneself as a unity. An immaterial person-substance is unnecessary because personal unity can be explained by a combination of (1) the persistence of the body-subject, (2) the persistence of basic patterns of conscious relations to objects and to other people, (3) the fact that consciousness is a continuing and temporally synthetic relation, and (4) the persistence of objects of consciousness. An immaterial ego could not be a sufficient condition of chronological unity, if Sartre is correct (as he seems to be) in claiming that the persistence of physical objects is an important and necessary ingredient in the experience of personal unity through time.

The arguments discussed above have been useful (even though Desan seems to misunderstand Sartre's position) since they represent the major traditional arguments in favor of the existence of immaterial subjects. Scanlon's arguments, though published more recently, are essentially similar to Desan's and therefore have been treated parenthetically. While Desan proceeds from Sartre's claim that consciousness is a relation, Scanlon bases his position on an examination of certain characteristics of unreflective and reflective consciousness. Scanlon tries to defend the claim that an investigation of reflection makes it "apodictically evident that any transcendental consciousness which constitutes a transcendent ego is itself a transcendental ego."[22] In support of this he says that reflection reveals a continuing subjective unity: a subject with individual characteristics and a "concrete intentional life" which is related to a continuing world of meanings.[23] But Scanlon does not take into account the fact that the body-subject can easily fulfill all of the conditions mentioned and that it is therefore superfluous to add a transcendental subject.

---

21. Philip Solomon et al., eds., *Sensory Deprivation: A Symposium Held at Harvard Medical School* (Cambridge, Mass.: Harvard University Press, 1961), p. 1.
22. Scanlon, "Consciousness," p. 351.
23. Ibid., p. 347.

Sartre's answers to these arguments represent a defense of his claim that it is unnecessary to multiply entities by positing the existence of an immaterial, nonspatial person-substance in addition to the body-subject.

It may be useful at this point to compare Sartre's position with the "no ownership" view of persons attacked by P. F. Strawson. Sartre's position is somewhat different from the position discussed by Strawson. The latter was unable to find a fully developed version of a "no ownership" theory, and it will be shown how Sartre's differs. The no-ownership view, as described by Strawson, includes Wittgenstein's alleged claim that "I" is used in different ways in "I have a toothache" and "I've got a bad tooth." Wittgenstein thought the latter use of "I" is interchangeable with "this body" but that the former use is not. Unlike the Cartesians, Wittgenstein thought the nonbodily use did not "denote a possessor." Strawson went on to say that since no ego was needed in thinking or in having pains, Lichtenberg wanted to substitute the impersonal "there is a thought" for "I think." Schlick, agreeing, added that the data of experience have no owner, unless one wishes to say, in a misleading way, that the body is the owner. This is the "no-ownership" view as Strawson describes it.[24]

Many of these points sound familiar from earlier discussion of Sartre, who would give a slightly different analysis of some of the uses of "I," although he would agree that "I" has different uses. He would distinguish between "I have a toothache," which mentions a reflexive awareness of a state of the body, and "I see a red patch," which is a reflective judgment about an act of the body-subject. He would not only agree that there are logically distinct uses of the word "I," but would agree that at least one of those uses refers quite strictly to the body: "in one sense the body is what I immediately am" (*BN*, 325). Sartre would agree that, in at least one sense, "I" does not denote a possessor; we saw that he described the ego as the object, not the owner, of reflective consciousnesses. Sartre uses the impersonal "there is consciousness of a chair" to describe direct, unreflective awareness of objects; he also uses "I think," but primarily at the reflective level.

Sartre's view of what is and what is not left "ownerless" should be clarified, and this will serve to distinguish Sartre's position from the one Strawson is attacking. The body, for

24. Strawson, *Individuals*, p. 90, n. 2.

Sartre, *is* ownerless (*BN*, 304). That is to say, the expression "my body" does not imply that there is an immaterial person which owns or is associated with this body, and which might conceivably change to another body. Sartre's arguments have been directed against the unnecessary multiplication of entities. The ability to say "my body" can be accounted for by the human capacity for reflection, that is, by our ability to take a semi-outside stance on ourselves. No owner is needed.

On the other hand, Sartre would not claim that *experiences* are unowned. This seems to suggest that experiences are things which might become detached and float away, or perhaps inhabit a consciousness-container which might become separated from the body and lost. Sartre, in arguing that consciousness is a relation, and in arguing that there is no need to posit the existence of a subject term of that relation other than the body, has tried to undercut whatever problem there might appear to be with respect to ownerless experiences. To speak of an experience is to say that some body-subject is intentionally related to an object, which may or may not exist. Since consciousness can be a reflexive relation, the object may be part of the body itself. There aren't any detachable entities—experiences—in this account.

Sartre would say that it is misleading to hold that experiences are unowned. At this point his position differs sharply from the view attacked by Strawson. Sartre says, however, that it is just as misleading to speak of experiences as "owned" (*BN*, 113–14). He would agree with Schlick, that is, that to call the body the "owner" of experiences is misleading. In support of Sartre, it can be said that the expression seems to be misleading for the following reasons.

What we own are possessions. To possess something is to stand in a certain kind of relation to that thing, legally or extralegally. However, we can be conscious of objects we do not possess, and can possess objects of which we are not aware. But we do not generally say that we can be conscious of objects we do not experience, nor do we say that we can experience objects of which we are not aware.[25] Furthermore, we can quite literally own something for a period of ten years, but we could not, except in a metaphorical sense, experience something

25. The exceptions would be "objects" which could not be owned at all: we could be conscious of mathematical truths, future ends, etc., but could not experience them.

for a period of ten years. Experiencing something and owning something seem to be two very different *kinds* of relation. If, on the other hand, the experiencing itself is supposed to be owned by the subject, this seems to be misleading in another way. It is comparable to saying that possessing is possessed by the subject. These considerations support Sartre's suggestion that it is a mistake to call the body the "owner" of experiences, or even to think that experiences have an owner.

Sometimes Strawson refers to the "no ownership" view by another expression, the "no subject" view.[26] The objections just made to calling the body the owner of experiences would not hold against speaking of the body as the subject of experiences. This, as we have seen, is just what Sartre maintains. The view that Strawson attacks, while similar to Sartre's in some respects, differs from Sartre's in the important respect that Strawson's "no ownership" theorist does not view experiences as having any subject at all. With this point in mind, Sartre's position can be clarified by contrasting it to Strawson's.

Strawson says that both the Cartesians and the defenders of the no-subject view hold that there are two uses of "I"; he adds that both are "profoundly wrong" in doing so. Sartre would agree with Strawson's attack on the Cartesian view that "I" refers at times to a body-substance, while it refers at other times to an immaterial thinking substance. Sartre's reasons for thinking it is unnecessary to posit the existence of the extra immaterial subject have already been given; his reasons for insisting on more than one use of "I" will be given later. Strawson's reason for saying that "I" cannot be used to refer to a "pure individual consciousness" is that this is a secondary concept which can only be analyzed in terms of the person-concept. Strawson claims that for states of consciousness to be ascribed at all, it is necessary that they be ascribed to the same things as corporeal properties; and both are ascribed to persons, he says.[28]

This suggests the central point of disagreement between Sartre and Strawson on the question whether persons could conceivably exist apart from the original body. Sartre could certainly agree with the Strawsonian point that a necessary condition of conscious relations' being ascribed is that they be ascribed to the same things as physical characteristics. Sartre's view of the spatially oriented nature of perceptual conscious-

26. Ibid., p. 90.
27. Ibid., p. 93.
28. Ibid., p. 98.

ness and the role of the "psychic" body in others' experience (still to be discussed) would suggest such agreement.

Sartre would argue, however, that Strawson's next point does not follow at all. It is unnecessary to suppose that some additional entity, the person, exists. Sartre has argued that both consciousness and physical characteristics can be ascribed to the human body itself.[29] Both Sartre and Strawson deny that persons could exist apart from bodies in general. But since Strawson thinks persons, rather than bodies, must be the owners of both conscious and physical attributes, he allows for the possibility that two persons could share the same body in alternation, or that a person could change to another body.[30]

Sartre's case for the inconceivability of persons' existing apart either from bodies in general or from the original body in particular rests on a two-stage argument. The first showed that it is unnecessary to multiply entities by positing the existence of an immaterial person-substance. The body itself can be the subject of conscious relations, as well as possess physical characteristics. No additional substance is needed. The second stage claims that it is inconceivable that the conscious body could exist apart from itself.

This line of argument can also be used against a different and more recent version of the change-of-body thesis. Jerome Shaffer has defended a Cartesian dualism, rather than the Strawsonian view that P-predicates (which pertain to conscious persons) and M-predicates (which pertain to material objects) are to be ascribed to the same entity. Shaffer claims it is conceivable that persons could change bodies; his basic reason is that it is a contingent fact that a body belongs to one person rather than to another person.[31] Sartre could argue that Shaffer begs the question. It is logically impossible that the conscious body could exist apart from itself; to claim that it is a merely contingent fact that a body belongs to one person rather than to another, Shaffer must have assumed that the person is something other than a thinking body. But that is what Shaffer intended to demonstrate.

Now, as we go beyond the question of logical possibility, consideration needs to be given to the moral implications of the

29. This suggestion is also made, but not developed, by Don Locke in *Myself and Others: A Study in Our Knowledge of Minds* (London: Clarendon Press of Oxford University Press, 1968), p. 143.

30. Strawson, *Individuals*, pp. 131–32.

31. Jerome Shaffer, "Persons and Their Bodies," *Philosophical Review*, 75, no. 1 (January 1966): 64.

question whether persons could change bodies. One of the traditional elements of the concept of persons has been the notion of moral accountability. Antony Flew has commented briefly on one difficulty faced by those who maintain that persons can survive physical dissolution: in such cases it would be difficult to know how one would identify persons for the purpose of holding them morally accountable.[32] A similar problem arises for those who hold that it is conceivable that persons could change bodies. Strawson admits that his discussion, which is addressed to the problem of individuation, does not settle the problems involved in reidentification of persons.[33] But reidentification of persons must surely be an essential part of holding persons accountable, if we are going to allow, as we must, that there are time gaps between promises and performances, between crimes and punishments.

For Sartre, bodily identity is a necessary condition of personal identity through time (*BN*, 309). The body serves as a necessary condition of personal identity somewhat differently for the individual himself and for others. For oneself, one's body is a continuing point of view on the world, the point from which perception originates and the center of action indicated by objects organized into an instrumental complex. For others, the human body can be reidentified by the same criteria that are applicable to other objects which have spatial characteristics. The role of the body in individuation is also mentioned by Sartre (*BN*, 310). In allowing the possibility that persons could change to other bodies, Strawson must be committed to the position that bodily identity is not a necessary condition of personal identity through time.

Some of the difficulties that follow from the Strawsonian position can be seen from the following case. In the first place, there seems to be no reason why, if persons could change bodies, they could not change to bodies of a different size, sex, and shape. The force of the example does not depend on this point, but it can be incorporated into the example to emphasize some of the problems. Let us suppose that Albert, a fifty-year-old, black haired, bearded wrestler, has strangled someone; to escape detection, his person changes to the body of blonde, smooth skinned, four-year-old Mary Jane.

32. Antony Flew, "The Question of Survival," in *Religious Belief and Philosophical Thought*, ed. William P. Alston (New York: Harcourt, Brace & World, 1963), pp. 382–83.
33. Strawson, *Individuals*, p. 131.

The first problem is what happens to Mary Jane's person (MJ-P)? The Cartesian might suppose that MJ-P refuses to leave Mary Jane's body (MJ-B). Does it make sense to speak of persons, as well as bodies, being strong? If MJ-P (as opposed to MJ-B) is as strong as Albert's person (A-P), then perhaps she can enforce this refusal, in which case MJ-B will be inhabited by both MJ-P and A-P. Assume now that a very clever detective has discovered the whereabouts of A-P, and has brought MJ-B before the judge—which person answers the judge's questions, MJ-P or A-P? If A-P deliberately tries to confuse the judge, either by remaining silent or by giving Mary Jane–like answers, how could the judge tell who answered or failed to answer?

The Strawsonian version of change of body will be slightly different. Strawson claims that M-predicates as well as P-predicates apply to persons. Since the point of Strawson's analysis is to make individuation possible, it must not be supposed that MJ-P and A-P can occupy MJ-B simultaneously. Since persons have corporeal properties, it may be that A-P brings his M-predicates with him when he changes to MJ-B. But how are A-P's M-predicates related to MJ-B's M-predicates?—for it would be silly to suppose that Mary Jane's vacated body ceases to have M-predicates. A-P has the M-predicates of being black haired, bearded, and six feet tall. When A-P changes to MJ-B, ousting MJ-P, presumably the new entity is six feet plus three feet tall, blonde and black haired, bearded and smooth skinned. This seems somewhat strange. Perhaps Strawson would say that A-P must have some corporeal characteristics, but that he can adopt totally new ones when he changes to his new body. If we assume that this is what Strawson intended, most of the problems which arise for the Cartesian also arise for Strawson.

Let us suppose that A-P is now the sole inhabitant of MJ-B, and that A-P has not kept his old physical properties but has adopted those of his new body, MJ-B. There is the problem of where MJ-P has gone. Has she been forced to enter A-B, or is she now disembodied, or has she inhabited a still different body? (In Strawson's view, only the first and third of these possibilities would permit us to count MJ-P as a person, rather than as a former person.)

The judge has a more direct problem. He faces MJ-B, who is inhabited by A-P, and asks questions about the murder. A-P answers truthfully in MJ-B's high-pitched voice: "I strangled the victim with my own hands." The judge, who happens to believe as most of us do, that the person is the bearer of responsibility, asks more questions. He receives answers which lead him to think that A-P, now speaking with MJ-B's voice, has the memories and character consistent with the assumption that A-P once inhabited A-B. The judge, now convinced that he is addressing the guilty person, A-P, says "Albert, show the court how you placed your hands around the neck of the victim, and how much pressure you used to kill him." At this point Mary Jane's fingers are placed on the neck of a dummy, and it is apparent to all that the fingers are neither long enough to have surrounded the neck of the victim nor strong enough to have exerted fatal pressure.

What does the judge do now? If he believes that persons could change to other bodies, and also believes that persons are morally accountable, then, since he has good reason to believe he is addressing A-P, and has had a legally acceptable confession from A-P, the only fair thing the judge can do is to punish the guilty person, A-P, even if the body now inhabited by A-P is incapable of performing the deed which was confessed to. The judge might consider that A-B ought to be punished also, since it was the fingers of A-B which actually closed around the neck of the victim. But the judge would immediately realize the possibilities for unfairness here, for A-B might now be inhabited by the innocent MJ-P, or by a completely different but innocent person, or by a person guilty of a lesser crime, or perhaps A-B has been abandoned by all persons.

The judge still has misgivings; perhaps the murder took place five years ago, and MJ-B did not even exist then. But he must punish the guilty person. He therefore makes the required judgment and commits Albert's-person-in-Mary Jane's-body to life imprisonment. Here, of course, additional problems arise. Does he commit MJ-B to the men's penitentiary, in keeping with A-P's character and crime? Or does he commit A-P to protective custody, in keeping with MJ-B's tender age? Given a life expectancy of seventy years, Albert, had he remained in his old body, would have had only twenty years to serve, whereas A-P (in MJ-B) is condemned to serve sixty-six years. This seems unfair, but one is not quite sure to whom.

The real problem now is that even if the judge could settle the question of guilt and punishment in a fair and consistent manner, there would be no reason to suppose that A-P would wish to, or would have to, remain in the body of Mary Jane for all those long years. A-P waits until sentence is passed, then changes back to his old body—or perhaps, if he is especially cunning, into the body of the judge—and lets MJ-B, which may or may not have been reinhabited by MJ-P, wait out the long sentence.

The point of this example is that if what we mean by persons is that they are not only perceivers but also moral agents, then it is not merely a small matter, causing occasional inconveniences in identification, to say that they might change to other bodies. Accountability has generally been held to be a part of the concept of a person, and moral accountability would be an inapplicable notion if persons were separable from the bodies with which they were originally identified. Persons are held accountable, for the most part, for acts, and morally relevant acts are usually considered to be actions taken by the body. If it were logically possible that persons could change to other bodies, then, by the same token, it would be logically possible that our entire machinery for establishing moral and legal guilt and innocence is unfair, unjust, and irrelevant.

This point should be distinguished from the rather different point that, in any given case of trying to establish guilt and innocence, it is logically possible that we make an error. Rather, what is being called into question is the entire institution of establishing guilt and innocence, and the related practices of punishment. What possible relevance would it have to establish that a certain body, X, was or was not at the scene of a crime on the night of that crime if his person might have been there or might have been absent, regardless of what his body was doing?

It is interesting to notice that one impetus for the attack on physicalism has been that the strict physicalist, who claims that the person is no different from any material object, undermines the notion that persons are morally accountable. It seems that an opposing position, namely, that persons are substances which could change to other bodies, leads to precisely the same difficulty. This can be offered as an additional, although inconclusive, consideration in support of the strong inseparability thesis defended by Sartre, and in opposition to the weaker Strawsonian inseparability thesis: moral accountability would be an inapplicable notion if persons could change to other bodies. It is possible that the change-of-body thesis would enjoy less favor than it seems to if the strong epistemological emphasis of current discussions were supplemented by more discussion of persons as moral agents.

In summary, the assumption that bodily identity is a necessary condition of personal identity is deeply embedded in legal and moral institutions and practices which are considered very important to Western civilization. This alone is not a conclusive reason, however, for saying it is logically impossible that persons could exist separately from bodies in general or from the original body in particular. Sartre's fundamental argument in favor of that thesis is given in two stages. First, since the conscious body can itself fulfill all the traditional roles of the immaterial subject, it is unnecessary to multiply entities by positing the existence of an immaterial ego in addition to the body-subject. Thus Sartre has shown that the conscious body can provide an existing, thinking center of action; can provide spatial and chronological unity; etc. No transcendental ego is needed. Second, it is logically inconceivable that the body-subject could exist apart from itself.

There is one other version of the change-of-body thesis which should be mentioned briefly, since Sartre would find this case problematic. The reason why he would find it a problem, however, is that the case does not really pose the classic question, whether persons could exist separately from their original bodies. Shoemaker discusses the example of a brain-transfer case: Brown's brain, transplanted into Robinson's body, can be called Brownson. Shoemaker thinks that if Brownson exhibits the memories of Brown, then we would, in all likelihood, say that he is Brown.[34]

The case is especially interesting in light of recent developments in transplantation of organs; it is certainly not inconceivable that, some time in the future, brains might also be transplanted. If Brown had been a fifty-year-old wrestler, and had strangled someone prior to the operation, then some (although not all) of the problems that arose in the Albert–Mary Jane example would arise in this case. Our present methods for determining moral accountability simply would not be adequate in a case like this; and the point emphasizes the extent to which we now depend on the assumption that bodily identity is a necessary condition of personal identity.

A few comments can be made on Shoemaker's case, in connection with Sartre's point that the body is conscious. It might be asked whether it is really plausible to assume, as Shoemaker does, that Brownson's memories would be unequivocally those of Brown. Ordinarily, many of our memories are memories of physical actions we have been trained to perform. Suppose that Brownson remembers very clearly that he used to grind lenses but finds, when he tries to handle the instruments, that his fingers are utterly unfamiliar with the techniques of using them. Or suppose that Brownson knows he never learned a certain complicated dance step but now discovers, when he

34. Shoemaker, *Self-Knowledge and Self-Identity*, pp. 23–25.

hears a certain piece of music, that his new feet move in an unfamiliar pattern.

In these cases we might wonder whether we were really dealing with Brown and Brown's memories, and whether we were dealing, instead, with hybrid memories and a hybrid person, Robinson-Brown. The question is empirical, but it seems much more plausible, in the absence of experiments, to assume that in a brain-transfer case, memories would reflect the confused nature of a hybrid body, rather than clearly reflect the memories of the brain portion of that hybrid.

Sartre could insist, in this example, that the fundamental issue, whether it is logically possible that persons could exist separately from their original bodies, does not arise in this case—as it would in Locke's celebrated prince-cobbler case—since that important part of the original body, the brain, has not been left behind.

The example raises another important question, however. It has frequently been thought that memory and character could serve as criteria of personal identity; and Sartre's claim that the body is the subject of conscious experiences does not exhaust the possibilities. Bodily identity is a necessary condition but, as we will see, not a sufficient condition of personal identity. Sartre thinks that, in one sense, "I" refers strictly to the body. But he is also committed to the claim that "I" is ambiguous. The reasons for insisting on other uses of "I" become apparent when we turn to his discussions of memory, character, and the ideal self.

Chapter 3

Persons and Memory

For Sartre, consciousness is not a substance, nor a container filled with mental contents placed inside an insentient body. Rather, consciousness is one basic form of relation that human bodies have to existent and nonexistent objects.

Sartre's concept of a person is ambiguous. In addition to the body (*qua* physical object and *qua* subject of conscious relations), Sartre says that part of what we mean by "person" is the pattern or system of intentional relations as they develop through time. "Man is no other than a series of undertakings ... he is the sum, the organization, the set of relations that constitute these undertakings."[1]

This chapter and the next will be concerned with the past elements of this system of relations, as known by the individual himself and by others: memory and character. The discussion of Sartre's concept of memory will be directed toward two problems: the idea of accountability, and reidentification of persons. One key distinction underlies his handling of both these issues. Sartre claims that remembering is partly objective and partly interpretive. Connected with this distinction is the idea that remembering is a form of intentional activity. It will be necessary to clarify this distinction before dealing more directly with the questions mentioned.

Remembering: Interpreting as Well as Certifying

Sartre's distinction may be developed in the context of certain claims commonly made by philosophers who discuss memory.

1. Jean-Paul Sartre, "Existentialism Is a Humanism," trans. Philip Mairet, in *Existentialism from Dostoevsky to Sartre*, ed. Walter Kaufmann (New York: Meridian Books, 1957), p. 301.

Most contemporary discussion of persons has an epistemological bent. The accuracy and objectivity of memory are frequently mentioned; and the usual way of analyzing memory claims is to emphasize their relation to past and present knowledge claims.

For instance, Norman Malcolm defines factual memory in the following way. "A person, B, remembers that p from a time, t, if and only if B knows that p, *and* B knew that p at t, *and* if B had not known at t that p he would not now know that p."[2]

Sydney Shoemaker defends as a necessary truth the proposition that our confident and sincere perceptual and memory statements are generally true.[3] He says that one's remembering of a past event seems, to oneself, "a brute, unanalyzable fact."[4]

B. S. Benjamin suggests that " 'I remember p' might, in part, be paraphrased 'p is true (or this performance is an instance of p) and you have *my* word for it.' "[5] Benjamin maintains that "remember," like "know," is a "certificatory concept," but that, unlike "know," one can use "remember" only to certify past-related statements or performances.[6]

Sartre could probably accept the foregoing claims with respect to the objective element in remembering; our memory of "brute facts" could certainly be stated in the form of knowledge claims about past events (*BN*, 497). However, Sartre is more interested in calling attention to a characteristic of remembering that is known to all of us, and is described in psychological experiments, but is generally ignored in philosophical analyses. To remember is not only to certify, although it is that in part; to remember is also to interpret the past (*BN*, 498). Sartre is not claiming that these are two distinct forms of memory, in the sense that one must be doing one or the other kind of remembering, but not both. He claims, rather, that both factual and interpretive elements enter into all types of remembering, whether it is remembering that something is the case or remembering having seen or done something.

The first problem is to clarify what Sartre means by saying memory is partly interpretive.

The following is offered as an analysis of Sartre's claim that

2. Norman Malcolm, "A Definition of Factual Memory," in *Knowledge and Certainty: Essays and Lectures* (Englewood Cliffs, N.J.: Prentice-Hall, 1963), p. 236.

3. Shoemaker, *Self-Knowledge and Self-Identity*, p. 239.

4. Ibid., p. 152.

5. B. S. Benjamin, "Remembering," in *Essays in Philosophical Psychology*, ed. Donald F. Gustafson (Garden City, N.Y.: Doubleday, 1964), p. 188.

6. Ibid., pp. 188–89.

"I remember p" contains an element of interpretation. His first move might be to ask for a more definite specification of p. A description of p might show it to be simply a brute fact. It is more likely to be the case that the description will show it to be an interpreted fact, if actual instances of remembering are described. Let us try the following descriptions of p, based on one of Sartre's examples (*BN*, 497).

p_1 : "I had whooping cough when I was five years old."

p_2 : "The one and only disease I ever had was that silly child's disease, whooping cough, when I was five."

p_3 : "When I was five years old and helpless, I was overwhelmed by that terrible and painful illness, whooping cough; my mother had to do everything for me for weeks afterwards."

p_4 : "When I was five I had whooping cough because my sister, who hated me, got into bed with me after she got whooping cough."

There is a common remembered fact in each of these descriptions of p; that is, I had whooping cough when I was five. Assuming that p actually happened, nothing we now do can change that past event, Sartre said (*BN*, 116, 497). If all or most of our remembering were a correct remembering of brute facts like p_1, then Benjamin and others might be justified in describing memory as a certificatory concept. Sartre's point is that most of our actual remembering is in fact more accurately described in ways suggested by p_2 through p_4.

Another way of putting this might be to say that "I remember p" is, factually speaking, generally elliptical for "I remember p as." The "as" suggests that brute facts are usually remembered as fitting within some system of interpretation. Let us see how this point is connected with Sartre's contention that memory is intentional; that is, it entails at least an implicit reference to a chosen future end, an end which may radically change.

It should be noted that the p-descriptions are not mutually exclusive; in fact, any one of them might count as a description of the very same case of whooping cough. The descriptions are brief enough and different enough that it is hardly plausible to suggest that any one of them is a complete description of the whole illness. This must mean that many properties of the events connected with the case of whooping cough have been left out of each description and have presumably been forgotten by the person who remembers the illness under description p_2 or p_3. But why did the individual, in one case, pick out the fact that this was the only disease he had ever had, while in the other case the sense of humiliation over being helpless is emphasized?

It might, of course, be possible to say that it is simply a matter of chance, which of the numerous properties of the period of illness are remembered and which are forgotten. Sartre does not think so. He agrees with the associationists and the Freudians insofar as they claim that a definite principle of selection operates in memory. He disagrees with them, however, on the nature of that principle. The associationist principle will be discussed in connection with B. F. Skinner's position.

Sartre's arguments against Freud are relatively sketchy but they can be set forth as follows. First, Sartre claims that the Freudian account is incoherent. The Freudian would claim that an unconscious complex, based on a childhood trauma, operates as a principle of memory selection. Certain memories, too painful to be borne, are repressed and unconscious, but they remain causally active with respect to present action. The conceptual difficulty, according to Sartre, is that the Freudian memory model requires a conscious unconscious. This is seen most clearly when a patient undergoing analysis offers resistance when his underlying complex is approached. If the complex is genuinely unconscious and thus barred from consciousness, how could the patient recognize that the complex is being approached? If the complex is thought to recognize itself, however, it is an unconscious which can understand, and is therefore conscious (*BN*, 573-74). But this is incoherent.

Sartre admits that real enlightenment can be attained through psychoanalysis. His own distinction between prereflective and reflective levels of behavior is intended to provide a more adequate conceptual framework than the Freudian idea of an unconscious. For Sartre, a patient can attain reflective knowledge of the objective patterns of his own thinking and acting, where before he had simply lived his life unreflectively. But Sartre insists that this, as well as the patient's resistance, is "truly understandable only if the subject has never ceased being conscious of his deep tendencies" (*BN*, 574).

An additional argument is that Freud may not in fact have carried his own research far enough. Sartre suggests this when he refers to the work of the psychiatrist Stekel, who claimed that in all cases which he had been able to investigate fully, he had discovered that "the crux of the psychosis was conscious" (*BN*, 54).

In distinguishing different levels of consciousness, and also distinguishing objective from interpretive remembering, Sartre hoped to provide a substitute for the incoherent Freudian concept of an unconscious barrier to memory. Our task is to see how Sartre accounts for the differences in the way the illness is remembered, if it is assumed that the same case of whooping cough might have been correctly remembered and described in any of these ways.

For Sartre, the principle of selection of remembered properties is in fact the same fundamental project the individual uses in selecting and organizing properties of perceived objects into an intelligible situation or instrumental complex (*BN*, 499–500). To the extent that an individual's past and present thoughts and actions exhibit a coherent pattern, Sartre believes it is because the individual has chosen an ideal self or fundamental project in life. The actions and ideas of an individual have a certain coherence, over a period of time, due to their being directed toward a particular fundamental goal.

The individual's perceptions, as well as his memories, reflect this choice of a future end. For instance, one may compare the ways in which a botanist and a poet perceive the same flower. To view the flower as the botanist views it is to see it as having a certain type of leaf and root system and as belonging to a particular species that requires certain soil and moisture conditions. The botanist may have ignored the color of the flower as irrelevant for his purposes. The poet, however, may consider the color of the flower as its outstanding property—its bright yellow against the gray-green background of the field makes the flower a symbol of hope in an otherwise dreary world, from the poet's point of view. Both men see the real flower, but they see it differently. Both men select certain genuine properties of the flower, and ignore other properties, depending on their purposes in looking at the flower. Neither man invents his perceptual experience, but each organizes the experienced properties differently.

To remember an event is also to make a selection among a large number of properties of the actual past event. Sartre can account for the differences in the *p*-descriptions in the following way.

Suppose that my fundamental goal in life is to become a strong and independent person. When I recall my early life, what I recall most vividly are those incidents which are connected with the themes of independence and strength, dependence and weakness. My memories of beautiful things are faint; memories of funny things that happened are unimportant. What is important for me are those remembered events which have a special connection to my chosen end.

I might remember my childhood case of whooping cough under description p_1 or p_3; both of them are connected, although differently, with the fundamental project I have chosen. The difference between them might represent different stages of my progress toward my end, or different moods. If I am already reasonably independent, I can remember with satisfaction that I was ill only once. If I am doubtful whether I really am independent, I might recall my early case of whooping cough as a period when I was painfully helpless; it might appear to have been a critical turning point in my life. It was then that I decided I would never lean on anyone again.

It might be, on the other hand, that I had enjoyed being helpless in bed. Depending upon whether my present project is to be independent or to get other people to do as many things to serve me as I can, I might remember the whooping cough under description p_3 with embarrassment or with satisfaction. The complication that is introduced in this case is that a complete description of an instance of remembering-as may entail reference to more than one end. Events which were once understood in one way can thus be later understood within a wholly different system of interpretation.

Sartre is suggesting, perhaps, that there are duck-rabbits of remembering, as well as duck-rabbits of seeing. One difference between seeing and remembering is that in remembering there is at least a double system of interpretation. We must take into account not only the instrumental complex within which p was originally experienced but must also mention the point of our present remembering. In some cases it might be necessary to take into account additional interpretive elements. The result is that brute facts may be forgotten or may assume a variety of appearances within various layers of interpretation. This is how Sartre accounts for the differences in p-descriptions (*BN*, 500).

There has been occasional contemporary discussion of interpretive elements in remembering, although philosophers have tended to assume that they are inaccuracies pure and simple. Thus, for example, Norman Malcolm claims there is a necessary connection between "I remember p" and "p is true." He then admits there are some (presumably vagabond) locutions, such as " 'that is how he remembers' " or " 'as he remembers,' " which permit us "to speak of incorrect memory."[7] It should be noted that Malcolm here considers only those characteristics of memory which are of epistemological importance: correctness and incorrectness. Thus he does not develop the notion of remembering-as or interpretation except in the context of a discussion of accuracy.

For Sartre, however, the reasons for distinguishing the interpretive from the objective aspects of memory are not primarily epistemological. The interpreted elements in remembering may be, for Sartre (unlike Malcolm), quite correct. Furthermore, the objective element in the memory report might be partly false (e.g., it might be that I had whooping cough when I was six rather than five).

However, it is not the correctness or incorrectness of memory with which Sartre is primarily concerned. Rather, he tries to give an account of the goal-oriented nature of our remembering, which provides a measure of coherence to the various items of our remembered past. As we will see, he connects this with his claim that we are morally accountable beings. He attempts to show how the intentionality of memory is linked to the particular selection of details remembered and forgotten. Whether or not these details are correct is another issue.

In any case, it should be clear that Sartre's distinction between the objective and interpretive aspects of memory cannot be assimilated to a distinction between what is and what is not correct, since either the objective or the interpretive elements of remembering may involve accuracies or inaccuracies in a given instance.

It is fair to ask what kind of support Sartre offers, or could offer, in behalf of his claim that memory is partly interpretive. Sartre does not argue for this position, except insofar as the facts themselves may be said to constitute an informal kind of argument in favor of a position. Since Sartre does not appeal to an *a priori* concept of remembering but intends, rather, to offer a description of the facts of remembering, he apparently considers the issue of whether memory is wholly objective to be a contingent question. Philosophers who discuss memory solely in terms of its certificatory function appear to be arbitrarily restricting the use of the term "remember." Factually speaking, however, the interpretive function of memory is just as impor-

7. Malcolm, "Memory and the Past," in *Knowledge and Certainty*, p. 189.

tant, and certainly just as frequently exercised, as the certificatory function.

Support for this point can be found in literary and autobiographical works (an example from the latter will be mentioned later). Even more significant, perhaps, is the support for Sartre's position which can be found in psychological experiments which seem, for the most part, to have been ignored by analytic philosophers who discuss memory. Sartre explicitly appeals to the work of the Gestalt psychologists (e.g., *BN*, 266). But other schools of psychology have also produced evidence for the prevalence of interpretation in our remembering.

For example, a psychologist-physician, Norman Cameron, has written a summary of experimental evidence that suggests that seeing and hearing include some distortions explicable in terms of the subject's purposes. Nor is remembering simply a recall of what has actually happened; it includes editing, no matter how honest and intelligent the witness is. To remember something is not just to repeat it but "to reconstruct, even sometimes to create, to express oneself" in reporting what one remembers.[8]

There is one line of argument, which Shoemaker presents, which might be used to cast doubt on Sartre's appeal to the facts of remembering. Shoemaker has argued that the proposition that our confident and sincere perceptual and memory statements are generally true is a necessary truth; this must be the case, since one could not establish this fact as a contingent truth without using observation and memory. But to do this would be to take for granted the very point one was trying to establish.[9] Shoemaker might argue, against Sartre, that there is something paradoxical about using empirical considerations to show that observation and memory statements are frequently interpretive, for one could show this only on the basis of observation and memory, and if one succeeded in showing it, one would have called into question the objectivity of the method by which one has shown it.

8. Norman Cameron, *Personality Development and Psychopathology: A Dynamic Approach* (Boston: Houghton Mifflin, 1963), p. 472. Cameron cites the following: F. Bartlett, *Remembering: A Study in Experimental and Social Psychology* (Cambridge: Cambridge University Press, 1932; F. Bartlett, *Thinking: An Experimental and Social Study* (New York: Basic Books, 1958); D.K. Kamano and J. E. Drew, "Selectivity in Memory of Personally Significant Material," *Journal of General Psychology* (1961), pp. 65, 25–32.

9. Shoemaker, *Self-Knowledge and Self-Identity*, pp. 234, 239.

The paradox is more apparent than real, however. The difficulty is that Shoemaker depends on a monolithic view of observation and memory. He overlooks the fact that science has progressed partly because of the use of instruments to make observations and to record results. Instruments can provide a check against fallible human powers: we can write down what we remember of a conversation and we can compare this with a tape-recording of that conversation. It is by such methods of checking that we are able to discover exactly the ways in which our memory statements are selective. The point is that Shoemaker takes too simplistic a view of methods if he claims that "observation and memory" cannot establish as a contingent truth that observation and memory statements are generally true—which is the claim he makes—or if he were to claim, contra Sartre, that "observation and memory" could not establish that observation and memory statements are not wholly objective. The scientist, in general, is trying to develop more precise and accurate methods, instead of imprecise and inaccurate methods, of observing and remembering. He is doing *this*, rather than pitting "observation and memory" against some unspecified nonobservational, nonremembering technique, as Shoemaker seems to assume.

The point of the foregoing remarks has been to show that there is empirical support for Sartre's contention that memory is partly interpretive, and to show that there is nothing really paradoxical about using such support.

In concluding this section of the discussion I would like to call attention to three points which have a special bearing on the concept of accountability.

First, Sartre would challenge Benjamin's claim that memory statements represent present knowledge of wholly past-related events. This is an oversimplification, comparable to saying that perception relates solely to the present. It was pointed out earlier that Sartre claims perception is a temporally synthetic act: to see object x *as* object x is in part to recognize it in comparison with memories of earlier sightings of x and to expect it to figure in future sightings in certain predictable ways. We also see x within an instrumental complex; that is, we see it as connected with some future end.[10]

10. Malcolm also suggests that remembering can refer to future events, such as remembering that there will be an eclipse. His point is quite different from Sartre's, however, and his concern is with factual, not

While perceptual statements can be formulated—"I see p in the light of, or in order to, y," where y is the future end in terms of which the original instrumental complex is organized— a memory statement is more complicated. The latter might be formulated thus: "I remember 'seeing (doing, having, etc.) p in the light of, or in order to, y' in the light of, or in order to, z." Here y is the end in terms of which p was originally seen (done, had, etc.) while z is the end in terms of which the present remembering of the past event is performed; y may or may not be the same end as z, as was pointed out in the discussion of independence.

Second, when Sartre speaks of remembering as partly interpretive, he does not intend to cast wholesale doubt on the viridicality of memory. To be sure, he does not offer any precise criteria for separating the factual from the interpretive elements in remembered facts, and he suggests that this may not be possible (*BN*, 498). But to interpret is not necessarily to falsify. It is to select and to arrange those details which are of interest, whether we see and remember as botanists, poets, or historians. This is not necessarily the same as seeing or remembering incorrectly, as Malcolm suggested. It is really to see and to remember distinctly those properties of events which are of special concern to us in our capacity as purposive beings.

This selectivity is in part a way of making sense out of periods of time, a way of connecting past events with what we want to be. To remember certain things in a certain way, and to ignore or forget others, is to introduce a kind of esthetic order into the chaos of past events that we have witnessed. This point is connected with the idea of accountability in the sense that Sartre maintains that a situation, past or present, can act on the individual only to the extent that he comprehends it in a certain way (*BN*, 498). This connection will be spelled out in the next section.

Third, remembering is not simply a kind of pictorial or propositional regurgitation of what has happened in the past; the individual is not passive with respect to his memories. Remembering is something we *do*, not something that happens to us.[11] Part of our knowing and remembering is to be explained by the effects that external events have had upon us.

interpretive, remembering. See "Three Forms of Memory," in *Knowledge and Certainty*, p. 204.

11. Sartre, *Imagination*, pp. 44, 143, 146.

But knowing and remembering are also products of how we select and arrange that material. Sartre is making a semi-Kantian point here. He differs from Kant in his claim that the categories applied to our experience are individual and purposive, rather than universal and cognitive.

We not only interpret the past, we can also reinterpret the past; and to that extent we can have some measure of present control over the past. We are not, then, at the mercy of the past, and we cannot excuse present actions on the basis of inexorable memories of the past.

Persons are accountable moral agents. This is the main point of Sartre's distinction between the objective and the interpretive elements of remembering. His discussion of memory is directed against those psychological determinists who would claim that memories of the past compel or coerce present action and that men are therefore not responsible for their acts. The position of these psychological determinists would imply that there are no persons—if the idea of accountability is included, as it usually is—in the concept of a person.

Accountability

It should be apparent that memory is involved, in some sense, in such statements as "I promised to pay him the money" and "I meant to keep my appointment, but I overslept." The notion of accountability, which has been an integral part of our traditional concept of a person, depends in part on the agent's memory of his past actions and intentions, but also on others' memories of the agent's past actions and promises.

Certain ways of conceiving memory have been proposed, however, which suggest that persons are not responsible for their actions. For instance, B. F. Skinner claims that all of men's actions are "initiated by forces impinging upon the individual"—that men have no ability to make choices and that therefore it makes no sense to hold them responsible for actions.[12]   John Hospers, appealing to psychiatry and to associa-

12. B. F. Skinner, "Freedom and the Control of Men," *American Scholar*, 25 (Winter 1955/56): 52–53.

tionism, makes a similar point: external circumstances mold or make people what they are and control what they do. [13]

In these theories the function of memory, although not explicitly stated, appears to be to exert causal pressure on present action. One's memories are supposed to prevent one from behaving differently than one is now behaving, or to lead one to do things that one thinks one ought not do: "I would have been a much kinder person if my uncle had not beaten me regularly." Sometimes the view seems to be that memories of past events and actions determine character, and that character, rather than memories directly, produces present action: "I ran away just now because I am a coward." This particular version of psychological determinism will be discussed in the next chapter.

Sartre has frequently been interpreted as defending an indeterminist position. [14] However, he explicitly rejects both indeterminism and determinism as traditionally conceived; he adds that if he had to choose between them, determinism makes more sense (BN, 436–37, 452–53). His own position may perhaps be described as a form of compatibilism. He explicitly claims that in order to be considered responsible, the agent must cause his choices and acts. Sartre readily admits that the individual is confronted with a large number of givens, which include the individual's parents, country of birth, race, constitution, and objective elements of his past history and present environment. He denies, however, that the individual is merely a passive product of these givens.

There is one basic sense in which Sartre claims that we can, so to speak, disengage ourselves from those givens—and this is crucial for the notion of the individual as a responsible moral agent. We can detach ourselves from what is given in the sense of imagining a nonexisting state of affairs, and we can pose this as a future end to be actively sought among those givens which are now seen in the light of that end (BN, 478).

Sartre does not oppose determinism as such, but he does oppose those forms of psychological determinism which (a) view man as wholly passive with respect to prior and external events, and (b) claim that men are therefore not responsible for

13. John Hospers, *Human Conduct: An Introduction to the Problems of Ethics* (New York: Harcourt, Brace & World, 1961), p. 521.
14. E.g., Adam Schaff, *A Philosophy of Man* (New York: Monthly Review Press, 1963), p. 69.

what they do. Sartre deplores the "attitude of excuse" which underlies these claims (*BN*, 40).

Since B. F. Skinner has given an extended defense of the two claims opposed by Sartre, it will be convenient to develop Sartre's view of memory and accountability in the form of comparison and contrast between his views and those of Skinner. The two men appear to hold completely opposed positions with respect to man's capacity for freedom and responsibility. It is startling, therefore, to find that Sartre and Skinner share a great many assumptions (some of the most important of these will be mentioned). It will be argued that one key difference between them centers on their treatment of human purposes or intentions. Skinner attempts to account for these purposes or intentions solely in terms of the past, while Sartre insists that goals are directed toward an unrealized future, and also that the interpreted elements of the remembered past itself can only be understood in terms of one's future goal. An imaginary dialogue will be developed between Skinner and Sartre with respect to the element of interpretation in memory, as it affects the concept of accountability.

Skinner's attack on the traditional notion that men are responsible creatures rests on his claim that science requires, as a postulate, that men are not free. But there seem to be at least two different forms of this claim. At times, Skinner says he is attacking the indeterminist view of freedom.[15] He sees this as linked with the traditional dualist view which posits, in addition to a body, an immaterial subject or "homunculus."[16] Since Sartre has rejected an indeterminist view, and since he has also argued against the position that there is an immaterial subject, there is no need to comment further on this version of Skinner's attack on freedom and responsibility.

The second form of his attack on freedom comes from Skinner's attempt to construct the new scientific picture of what a human being is. (As we will see, there seem to be two significantly different versions of the "scientific view," one which supports and one which does not support the nonresponsibility claim.) What we discover, Skinner says, is not a person inside a body but rather "a body which *is* a person in the sense

15. B. F. Skinner, *Beyond Freedom and Dignity* (New York: Bantam/Vintage, 1972), p. 17; hereafter abbreviated *BFD* and noted parenthetically in the text.

16. B. F. Skinner, *Science and Human Behavior* (New York: Macmillan, 1953), p. 447; hereafter abbreviated *SHB* and noted parenthetically in the text. See also *BFD*, p. 191.

that it displays a complex repertoire of behavior" (*BFD*, 190). This much of Skinner's view is similar to what Sartre says about the conscious body-subject. Skinner, as well as Sartre, claims there is a sense in which the personality or self is "distinct from the body" (*BFD*, 5). In this sense, Skinner says the self is a *"functionally unified system of responses"* (*SHB*, 285). Skinner's definition is similar to Sartre's claim that the person is, in one sense, a pattern or system of relations which the body-subject develops through time. Both Skinner and Sartre remark on the relative coherence of this system of responses or relations, but they differ quite sharply in their attempts to account for this coherence.

Skinner, writing within the "blank tablet" empiricist tradition, sometimes sees man as a passive product of circumstances over which he has no control. Having abolished the free immaterial subject, Skinner says that "all . . . alternative causes lie *outside* the individual" (*SHB*, 447–48). Again, "a person does not act upon the world, the world acts upon him" (*BFD*, 202). Thus external circumstances and past events have given the individual system of responses its specific shape. All talk of goals is misleading since it appears to make reference to an effective future state; goals are to be explained, instead, in terms of past consequences (*SHB*, 87).

This particular version of the "scientific view" seems to be what gives support to Skinner's claim that man is not responsible. Let us call this the Passivity View and refer to "Skinner (PV)" when this particular group of assumptions is meant.

Unfortunately for the coherence of Skinner's "scientific picture" of man, he often describes operant behavior (as opposed to reflex activity) in such a way as to suggest that people are not merely acted upon. In addition, they "interact" with their environment (*BFD*, 16). Thus in one description of operant behavior he says that such "behavior *operates* upon the environment to generate consequences" (*SHB*, 65). Again, he says that operant behavior is *"emitted, rather than elicited"* (*SHB*, 107). He considers his version of behaviorism to have progressed far beyond the early behaviorist notion of man "as a push-pull automaton" (*BFD*, 193),[17] although the Passivity View certainly suggests that he has not fully escaped that tradition.

Skinner agrees with Sartre that our seeing and remembering

17. Many of Sartre's objections to the associationist model of memory revolve around his claim that it is too mechanistic. See, e.g., *Imagination*, pp. 20, 49, 11.

are selective and that they exhibit a coherence. Operant discrimination does not depend simply on external or prior stimuli but on a quite different set of factors: "operant reinforcement and deprivation" (*SHB*, 272). Skinner notes that there is no way of "identifying a reinforcing stimulus as such" prior to testing it on a given organism, and that no single verbal or nonverbal response can be controlled by any given stimulus (*SHB*, 84, 277). Thus many of Skinner's descriptions of operant behavior retain the individual within the causal series, but make him active within this world—and not simply a passive product of prior and external forces. Let us call this the Activity View and refer to "Skinner (AV)" when this group of assumptions is meant. (Skinner himself does not distinguish the two positions.)

Most of the remaining discussion of Skinner will be directed toward the Passivity View. There are several reasons, in addition to simple fairness, however, for attempting to spell out the Activity View. First, Sartre could probably agree with much of what Skinner says about operant behavior, except that Skinner leaves us with a mystery in attempting to account for the unpredictability of given stimuli in producing reinforcement, while Sartre can point to active human choice. More important in the present context is that there seems to be no good reason for Skinner to deny that people can be held responsible for operant behavior. If I "generate consequences," then surely I am accountable for these, and it comes as a small surprise to find that Skinner (AV) sometimes acknowledges this (e.g., *SHB*, 115). Even if there are additional causes at work within any given situation, I am accountable if my choice or my act is a necessary condition of y's occurrence or a necessary condition for preventing z's occurrence.

To return to the Passivity View, Sartre would insist that the scattered items in our past and present environment are too chaotic to account for the high degree of coherence in our responses to them. That coherence can be better explained by an account of the fundamental goal we have chosen. Not even the past can coerce us, since we actively choose our past in the sense that we interpret its meaning. This interpretive connection to the past makes it impossible to say that the past renders us nonresponsible for present actions. The differences between Sartre and Skinner (PV) can be more fully explored with respect to remembering as it pertains to accountability. Skinner's first move might be to attempt in some fashion to discount the interpretive element.

Let us take two examples of x, a present action which is, by hypothesis, connected in some way with the fact that I remember having had whooping cough when I was five. The question is whether Skinner (PV) is correct in claiming that that link must be conceived wholly in terms of past external events producing a present act.

x_1 : I am putting arsenic in my sister's tea.

x_2 : I just called my neighbor to help me put in a fuse; I keep forgetting how many appliances can be plugged in at one time.

Neither of these actions appears at first glance to be connected in any way with my memory of an illness when I was five years old. Skinner (PV) is not content with this. He is searching for the ultimate determinants of these present actions: so he questions the agents at length. He concludes that neither individual is responsible for his present action.

The reason for making the nonresponsibility claim in the case of x_1 is that the individual can produce a great many memories of the sort: "When I was five I had whooping cough because my sister, who hated me, got into bed with me after she got whooping cough." The reason for making the nonresponsibility claim in the case of x_2 is that the individual can produce a great many memories of the sort: "When I was little and helpless, I was overwhelmed by that terrible and painful illness, whooping cough; my mother had to do everything for me for weeks afterward." The Skinnerian psychological determinist shows us there is a connection, after all, between the apparently unrelated x_1 and the memory of whooping cough, and the apparently unrelated x_2 and the memory of whooping cough. The individual who attempts murder is ultimately blameless, since past external events beyond his control, among them whooping cough-resulting-from-sister's-hostility, have caused the feelings and motives which produce his present murder attempt.

Sartre would agree that there is *a* connection between present action and memories of past events. In fact, he insists that we often experience our past as compelling present actions (*BN*, 501). The question he would raise is whether the experienced connection is solely an objective causal connection of the sort that would render us passive in relation to the past and thus nonresponsible, as Skinner (PV) would claim. Sartre insists, to be sure, that we cannot make a decision which is wholly irrelevant to past events; we do not act in a vacuum (whatever that might mean) but act only in response to circumstances, past and present, which are actually given (*BN*, 496). But does this mean that those external and past circumstances must be viewed as the sole causes of our present action?

In the first place, Sartre would point out, Skinner could not have shown a connection between either of the present actions, x_1 or x_2, and the remembered brute fact, p_1; when Skinner succeeded in coming up with a connection, it was a link between present actions and interpreted remembrances, p_4 and p_3. The interpretation of past facts is not, however, an additional brute fact. It is a way of selecting certain properties of past events, of ignoring other properties of those same events, and of organizing them in such a way as to make sense of them.

There seem to be two basic moves which Skinner might make in reply. He might try to say that the interpretive element, while present, is superfluous in this case. (In the context of a different discussion, Skinner admits the existence, but not the relevance, of feelings [*BFD*, 12].) The other basic move might be to admit the relevance of interpretation, but to explain the interpretation itself in terms of past and external events. These alternatives will be explored in turn.

Suppose Skinner (PV) grants that an interpretive connection can be found in the example mentioned, but then claims that the interpretation is superfluous. The reason he might offer is that the example can be redescribed in such a way as to eliminate altogether the interpreted reference to whooping cough, and instead can speak of the entirely objective external past event, an "instance of hostility." Let us take the alleged causal law, "hostility breeds aggression," and predict that if there is a sufficient number of cases of hostility of sufficient strength, the individual who is the object of this hostility will probably commit some act of aggression.

Skinner (PV) might in this way argue his case, perhaps not by eliminating the interpretive element of remembering altogether but by claiming that it is irrelevant to the objective causal connection between present actions and memories of external past events.

Sartre can show that this move does not make the interpretation superfluous; it merely conceals the points at which certain facts have been selected as important and certain others ignored. The Skinnerian redescription of Sartre's example can be examined more closely to see how Skinner has made a selection of some properties and ignored others. The psychologist who speaks of an "instance of hostility" is abstracting a certain property, "hostility," from a complicated situation which would surely exhibit any number of additional properties in any given case. The whooping cough case seems to be a realistic example of a set of events which includes, among other properties, a sister's hostility in transmitting whooping cough. In describing this case as an "instance of hostility" Skinner (PV) would have picked a particular property of this set of events and ignored most of the others. The same procedure would have been at work in any description of an event or set of events as an "instance of hostility."

To support his claim that the individual who drops arsenic in his sister's tea is not responsible for his action because this act has been determined by memories of past instances of hostility, Skinner (PV) would have to show why the individual was compelled to remember only the hostility feature of those past events and to ignore all the other features. How does he account for the fact that the individual who commits action x_2 remembers the same set of events under the description p_3? In redescribing the whooping cough case as an "instance of hostility," Skinner (PV) would not eliminate the interpretation from consideration but would simply adopt one of the possible interpretations.

The difficulty is compounded when it is mentioned that the whooping cough case might have been much more complicated. It might well be that an additional property of this set of events was

p_5: "My sister brought me all her favorite toys when I was sick with whooping cough."

If I remember the illness under description p_4, and have forgotten the additional fact describable as p_5, then of course I can feel justified in my present act of aggression. Skinner (PV) is making the claim, however, that I really *am* blameless. It is not clear in this case just why he can make that claim, since the particular abstraction, "instance of hostility," would neglect the opposing evidence.

Suppose another complication. As we noted earlier, p_4 is an interpreted fact. If we try to separate out the objective element, we seem to be left with the brute fact that my sister climbed into bed with me after she got whooping cough. I interpreted this, at the time, as an intention on her part to make me ill. But perhaps this was a wholly mistaken interpretation. She was too young to understand that I might catch the disease, and was frightened at feeling ill; it was for comfort that she climbed into my bed. Describing the case as an "instance of hostility" is a way of ignoring the possibility of a real error in interpreting events. Surely, then, the Skinnerian psychological determinist has not eliminated the relevance of the interpretive connection by the simple ploy of adopting one of the interpretations, ignoring all of the other possible interpretations, and even, perhaps, ignoring some of the facts.

Skinner (PV) might attempt to defend the choice of the particular description he gave by pointing to the nature of the present action. He might argue that there was nothing arbitrary about calling this case an "instance of hostility" inasmuch as it was this property of the whooping cough case which had the causal strength, in combination with similar properties of other events, necessary to produce the murder attempt (cf. *BFD*, 14). Skinner (PV) could agree that perhaps there were many additional surrounding circumstances, but this would unquestionably be the case in any causal sequence. It would be silly to say it is "just a matter of interpretation" if we ignore the color of my shirt when we are trying to list the causes why a match burst into flame. Isn't it equally silly to say that all of those additional factors should be taken into account when what we are trying to explain is a present action, attempted murder, and when only a single property of the whooping cough example, hostility of a sister, is relevant in the sense of being part of a regularly recurring sequence?

The argument that the additional circumstances are causally irrelevant might be maintained in descriptions p_2 and p_3, but this cannot be true of the examples just given, description p_5 and the case in which I was mistaken about my sister's intention. In the latter, the connection between present action and past event is *purely* interpretive. It is my thinking, mistakenly, that my sister meant me harm that is supposed to be a cause of my present murder attempt. If I am mistaken, however, in believing that the matches are dry, my mistaken belief is not considered to be relevant. The matches will light only if they are really dry. In the case of description p_5, evidence of the sister's affection is clearly relevant to a discussion of whether or not past hostility compelled present action; but this part of the relevant evidence has been suppressed by the psychological determinist who claims I am not responsible.

What enables him to do this convincingly is that he is working backward from the action for which he wants to find a cause. If he had started by describing antecedent conditions, which would have included a number of events whose properties were similar to those in descriptions p_4 and p_5, he could not have predicted the particular action x_1, nor could he have viewed x_1 as the second event in a regularly recurring sequence of (p_4 and p_5), resulting in x_1. Once he knows what action he is trying to explain, the Passivist can make a case for finding external causes of that action by the expedient of using the action itself as a means of deciding which antecedents are relevant. But this is surely an empty device.

Sartre agrees that if we are to understand the connection between present action and remembered past events, the first thing to look at is the present action. But the reason for this is that there *was* no definite connection between antecedent conditions and any particular subsequent action until the present action was decided upon. Factually, a collection of past events merely exhibited a chaotic variety of properties. Sartre makes the rather startling point that the past's claims upon us should be stated as "hypothetical imperatives: 'If you wish to have such and such a past, act in such and such a way' " (*BN*, 503).

Sartre is not saying that we are able to change the brute facts of the remembered past; his point, rather, is that there is an element of choice in our remembering, contrary to what Skinner (PV) holds. We decide what our past means by acting in the present to achieve one kind of goal as opposed to some other kind of goal (*BN*, 498). What links present action to memories of past events is, at least in part, an interpretive connection which can only be understood in terms of the individual's chosen future end. Since a past illness can influence the individual's present acts only to the extent that he has some particular understanding of that situation, Sartre claims that the power to interpret past events means the remembered past cannot act upon us in such a way as to render us nonresponsible for our present actions (*BN*, 572).

Let us suppose another modification in Skinner's Passivity View, a modification which admits a relevant and important interpretive element in our memory of past events, as well as some end that connects memories of past events to present action. What makes it an example of the position Sartre criticizes is the added claim that the meaning of the past is fixed, and/or that the end is determined by external and past events.[18]

Sartre says that we choose our past in the sense that we select

---

18. Cf. Skinner (*BFD*, p. 184), who claims that recall is only an evocation of earlier responses. Also (*SHB*, p. 87), goal talk, he claims, can be reduced to past consequences. Also *SHB*, pp. 342–43, 428, 433.

certain features of past events, ignore other properties of those events, and organize them in such a way as to make sense of them in the light of our present ends. However, Skinner (PV) could argue that this is no different from what the cat does when it settles down by the fire to get warm. Here the cat also selects certain properties of its environment—primarily warmth—and ignores many others, such as the color of the wallpaper, to fulfill its "purpose" of getting warm. But no one would think that we should "hold the cat responsible" for settling down by the fire.

Skinner (PV) might point out that what Sartre calls a choice is exhibited even by plants: the corn plant selects certain nutrients from the soil and air, and fails to respond to a great variety of other elements in its environment. This "selection" is made on the basis of what contributes to the survival and growth of the plant, but again there is no temptation to believe the plant is making a choice. Even an inanimate object, such as a barometer, might be described as responding selectively to its environment. So even if Sartre is correct in claiming that we select some properties and ignore others in our perceiving and our remembering, and even if the selection is made in order to serve some end, Sartre has not convinced us that human beings are thereby doing something that cannot be done by animals, by plants, and by certain material objects.

Even if the opponent is willing, then, to admit that remembering is partly interpretive, in the sense of being a meaningful "selection" of certain properties of past events, he could claim that we have no control over that meaning. The environment itself has determined that "selection" (*BFD*, 14). Skinner can claim that the individual is not responsible for the attempted murder, or even for a successful murder, since he could not help selecting as meaningful those instances of hostility which determine his present purpose of killing his sister— any more than the cat could help selecting the fire's warmth as the property which moved it.

Sartre offers two objections to the Passivist version of psychological determinism just described. First, he says that the meaning of a given event or type of event varies from individual

---

Skinner adds the curious point that whatever is to be found in action beyond past experience is "guessing" (see *SHB*, p. 436).

Presumably, when Skinner urges that a state of affairs similar to that described in *Walden Two* ought to be brought into existence, he is not asking us to choose such a state of affairs but is guessing that it might happen (or that it will happen?).

to individual. Second, the meaning of one's own past as a whole can be suddenly and completely reinterpreted in the light of a newly chosen end (*BN*, 573). Both points can be discussed.

Sartre would first insist on the point brought out in earlier examples, that the meaning of a case of whooping cough, for example, can be quite different for one individual than its meaning for other individuals. This point is closely connected with the fact that there are no fixed ends for human beings (i.e., "existence precedes essence" [*BN*, 566–68]).[19] The point Skinner (PV) has overlooked is that cats and corn plants cannot imagine and choose from a variety of possible ends. If we speak of animals' and plants' "selecting" certain properties of their environment and "ignoring" others, it is in quite a different sense than when we speak of human beings' selecting and ignoring certain properties of their environment and their past. The selectivity exhibited by human beings is of a different kind, and cannot be explained in terms of a common human nature plus certain external circumstances.

Sartre appears to base this claim on an informal appeal to facts. What he seems to have in mind is that in the human world, unlike the cat world, any given object may be either a matter of indifference or extremely significant. Furthermore, the particular kind of significance that an object, seen or remembered, can have, varies from individual to individual, and for one individual at various times. But if the external environment determines what we select as meaningful (which seems to be what Skinner [PV] has in mind when he says the environment "selects" [*BFD*, 14; *SHB*, 433]), it ought to operate uniformly on all people. Money, however, can be an object of utter indifference or deep significance. It may be important in its own right, or as a symbol of something else, or primarily as a means to some end. It may be loved or loathed, or an object of moral disapproval. The point is that Skinner (PV) cannot support a claim that the external past circumstance of poverty, for instance, is causally connected with any specific subsequent actions, since money and lack of money can mean completely different things to different people.

One argument, then, against a Passivity View that would admit an interpretive element into our seeing and our remembering, but would maintain that the interpretive element is itself fixed and determined by external circumstances, or by the past, is simply to point out that the facts do not seem to lend

19. Cf. supra, ch. 1, n. 52.

themselves to this interpretation. Sartre uses this line of argument against the Freudians' claim that there are "elementary symbolic relationships (e.g., the faeces = gold, or a pincushion = the breast) which preserve a constant meaning in all cases" (*BN*, 573). There is too much variety in the properties human beings respond to, and too much variety in the responses themselves, to support a claim that fixed meanings are attached to given properties of objects seen or remembered.

Curiously, Skinner (AV) agrees with this. He insists that operant discrimination is distinct from a mere conditioned reflex (*SHB*, 271). He points out that operant behavior "is not elicited by current stimuli and does not depend upon the previous pairing of stimuli" (*SHB*, 272). He refers, rather, to "operant reinforcement and deprivation" as the "primary controlling variables" in such cases. Prior to testing on a given individual, he says, there is no way of identifying a reinforcing stimulus as such (*SHB*, 84).[20] In other words, Skinner (AV) apparently abandons one of the important claims within his Passivity View in the course of some of his discussions of operant behavior. Thus it is not always the case that the individual is controlled by external and prior circumstances.

Skinner is clearly uncomfortable with this, however; he attempts to salvage his nonresponsibility claim by suggesting that there is "perhaps" a biological explanation for the aforementioned variety of responses to various stimuli. But some of Skinner's illustrations fail to support such a suggestion. For example, he speaks of someone who is frequently engaged in thinking about and looking for four-leaf clovers. He mentions another example: someone who is extremely interested in dogs, and goes out of his way to pursue this interest (*SHB*, 271). It does not seem plausible to give a biological explanation for either interest. Sartre claims it makes more sense in such cases to say that the individuals are pursuing certain chosen goals which lend a coherence and intelligibility to that behavior.

At this point Skinner will try to revert to the Passivity View. If he were to concede Sartre's point that the meanings involved make sense only in relation to certain goals, he would insist that

20. With this admission Skinner may in fact abandon determinism as it is usually defended by contemporary philosophical determinists. Bernard Berofsky has emphasized that for the determinist, "all events (facts, states) are lawful in the sense, roughly, that for any event *e*, there is a distinct event *d* plus a (causal) law which asserts, 'Whenever *d*, then *e*.' " Bernard Berofsky, editor's introduction to *Free Will and Determinism* (New York and London: Harper & Row, 1966), p. 6.

these goals are themselves determined by the external conditions of our environment or by society or by memories of past events (*SHB*, 343). There is no reason to suppose that we can choose any of the ends toward which we move; they have been programmed into us. Thus the individual is ultimately nonresponsible for his own actions (*SHB*, 229).

Sartre's reply is to point to those rare cases of a "radical conversion," cases in which external past and present conditions remain constant but the individual suddenly abandons his previous choice of a fundamental end in favor of a new one (*BN*, 573). Although these cases are rare, they represent a permanent possibility for each of us, Sartre claims. Most of the time people ignore or try to hide from themselves the possibility of adopting a radically different purpose in life; they enjoy the security of thinking they cannot help pursuing the ends they now pursue. This is the case whether they are good, solid citizens who find it disturbing to think that they might, after all, commit a murder or embezzle the company's funds, or whether they are town drunkards enjoying the comfortable belief that they cannot help reaching for that bottle. The recognition that I have chosen the basic end I now pursue, and that I might choose a completely different end at any instant, is accompanied by anguish, Sartre says (*BN*, 32).[21]

The example of Malcolm X may show why Sartre thinks actual and possible "radical conversions" can be used in an argument against the Passivist's claim that the ends we pursue are determined by past and external events. Sartre does not spell out what he means, but perhaps his point can be argued as follows. The difficulty Sartre seems to refer to is that Skinner (PV) is faced, in some cases of radical conversion, with a situation that appears to be formulable in the following way:

$$c_1, c_2, c_3, \ldots, c_n \text{ cause } E$$
$$\text{and}$$
$$c_1, c_2, c_3, \ldots, c_n \text{ cause } not\text{-}E$$

C_1 through c_n represent all the prior and external circumstances of the individual's life and E represents an end which is

21. There is an inconsistency in what Sartre says here. He appears to claim that at least one fixed meaning, anguish, is attached to the recognition of the possibility of a "radical conversion." It would seem to be more consistent with his attack on the Freudian claim, that there are universal symbolic meanings, if Sartre were to say that the recognition of the possibility of a personal radical conversion might mean different things to different people. For one person it might lead to anguish, for another it

supposed to be determined by those circumstances. However, Skinner (PV) must claim that *not-E*, the suddenly adopted new end, is determined by precisely the same set of external and prior conditions. What is described here cannot be a sufficient description of a causal relation. Sartre would claim that the abrupt change of ends can only be explained by introducing the agent's choice into the account as an additional condition.

In the case of Malcolm X, the basic goal beneath the actions and thoughts of his early life was this: E = emulation of the white man. While he pursued this project, his new acquaintance with an Americanized version of Islam did not interest him. It is this point that Sartre would emphasize if the Skinnerian Passivist tried to claim that the externally initiated introduction to Islam determined his new end: *not-E* = rejection of the model of the white man. It was, rather, his act of adopting the new end which produced the change in his attitude to Islam, when Malcolm X discovered that Islam provided him a framework of religious beliefs within which the white man is depicted as a devil.[22] If the Passivist were correct in claiming that E was not subject to the person's control, E would have caused Malcolm X to reject the doctrines of Islam, as he did at first, and as he might have continued to do.

Since Skinner (PV) claims that human ends are externally determined without reference to the agent's choice, it is fair to ask him to formulate a uniform set of antecedent conditions which could produce a particular end. If we take the preaching of Christianity as an example of a basic project, there seems to be only one necessary condition that would be present in all cases of someone's adopting this end: the person is acquainted with Christian teachings. This antecedent condition would be shared, of course, by someone whose fundamental end is to refute Christian doctrine.

It is, in other words, too general a condition to be of any assistance in trying to formulate a causal sequence. It is a little like saying that a necessary condition of an earthquake is that there be an earth. If we try to isolate specific antecedent conditions common to cases of purposing to preach Christianity, none can be mentioned. There may or may not have been a

---

might mean an exhilarating possibility, while for still another person this might be primarily food for philosophical thought. This inconsistency does not affect his claim that there are radical conversions, however, or that they are possible even where they do not occur.

22. *The Autobiography of Malcolm X*, assisted by Alex Haley (New York: Grove Press, 1965), p. 197.

Christian upbringing; there may or may not have been a previous life of crime; there may or may not have been a family
tradition of preaching, or of business ventures or piracy. In the
absence of uniform sets of antecedent conditions, it is difficult
to see how the conviction that ends are externally determined
could be supported. Sartre might have used this argument
against the Passivity View.

Sartre's argument against the claim that ends are determined
by external circumstances, however, is that even if an individual
maintains his choice of a fundamental project throughout his
life, he might at any time imagine a state of affairs other than
the one toward which he aims, and might revoke his original
choice in favor of a new one, without any alteration in the
external events. It is in the case of a radical conversion, or the
possibility of it, then, that we see most clearly why Sartre
thinks the choice of fundamental ends is not determined by
past and external forces impinging on a passive individual.

One final point should be made concerning the radical conversion. In such cases there is not only a change of fundamental
purpose but a change in the entire framework of meaning which
is organized in terms of that purpose. Past events cannot determine our present actions, not only for the reasons mentioned—
that we can select which of the innumerable features of the
present and past environment to respond to and, furthermore,
can select among various possible responses to those features—
but also because we can make a new response to those same
properties of objects and events in the light of a new end. What
was remembered as a duck can be suddenly remembered as a
rabbit. Sartre says that it is always possible to change the
meaning of the past, to the extent that it was goal-oriented,
even though the actual events of the past remain beyond control (*BN*, 116).

A simple example of this is the change of meaning Malcolm X
attached to "conking" his hair, that is, giving it a painful lye
treatment in order to straighten it. He describes the details of
his first "conk" job, and his sense of self-admiration at the pain
endured and at the transformation of his hair, so that it was "as
straight as any white man's."[23] At the time, he perceived his
straight hair with pride, in the light of his end, which was to
emulate the white man. That is, he perceived h in the light of E.

Later rememberings of this "conk" job could be expressed in
the formula Malcolm "remembered 'doing h in the light of E' in

23. *Autobiography of Malcolm X*, p. 54.

the light of z" where the present end, z, might be the end E—as it was for a certain period of Malcolm's life. When E was replaced by *not-E*, it was not only that Malcolm X rejected future actions which took the white man as a model; by the same choice he transformed the meaning of his past. Here we are dealing with only a tiny fragment of his past, h. When z was transformed from E to *not-E*, h took on a wholly different meaning in the light of this new end.

Malcolm later remembered this painful hair treatment as a degrading experience, suffered for the sake of an end he came to feel was ridiculous.[24] There was no alteration of the objective past event to which the remembering referred, but there was a radical change in the interpretation of that event.

Sartre would say that the memory of the hair straightening was transformed by being integrated into a new system of interpretation. Thus past events do not have a fixed and unalterable meaning for a given person, since he may view them differently in the light of new ends. The remembered past cannot, then, render the individual nonresponsible for his present actions. He is accountable for what he now makes of his past, as well as for what he projects for the future.

Reidentification

Memory has traditionally been thought to play an important role as a criterion of identity. Locke held memory to be a person's sole criterion of identity for himself;[25] and many others have thought that memory is so important a criterion of identity that it could override bodily identity in alleged change of body cases. If Sartre had discussed this particular question, he might have taken an approach similar to that of B. A. O. Williams, who agrees with Sartre that bodily identity is a necessary condition of personal identity. Williams contends that the attempt to separate physical from "mental" criteria does not work, since the use of mental criteria involves the bodily criterion. For instance, one could not distinguish cases of seeming to remember something from cases of really remembering some-

24. Ibid.
25. John Locke, *An Essay Concerning Human Understanding*, annotated by Alexander Campbell Fraser (2 vols.; New York: Dover Publications, 1959), vol. 1, bk. II, ch. 27, p. 449.

thing unless one could refer to the body's presence at the scene of events the individual claims to remember.[26] While Sartre might have taken a similar line of approach if he had discussed the question whether the memory criterion could override the bodily criterion, the question does not arise within the position he developed since it would be logically impossible for the body-subject to change to another body.

There is another way in which Sartre is concerned with memory and reidentification, however. His position might be paraphrased by saying that while there could not be more than one body per person, there could be more than one person per body. Sartre claims that "I" is ambiguous. In one sense the person is a body *qua* conscious subject. In another sense, a person is the pattern or system of conscious relations that this body has with objects and with others through time. There might be more than one person per body, in the sense that a particular body-subject might develop a wholly new pattern of relations to the world and to the people around him, as in radical conversion. Sartre could describe multiple personalities as alternating patterns of relationships.

The use of memory in reidentification of persons would reflect the ambiguous nature of the concept of person. For Sartre, memory performs both a certificatory and an interpretive function. In the sense in which a person is a continuing body-subject, he can be reidentified by his memory of brute facts to which this body was witness. In the sense in which the person is a pattern or system of relations to objects, he can be reidentified *or* discovered to be no longer existing, depending upon whether there is continuity or discontinuity in the interpretive element of remembering.

A good example of this part of Sartre's distinction between these two ways of reidentifying persons is a passage written in prison by Malcolm X, just after he had become deeply interested in Islam. He remembered, as if it had been lived by "someone else," the life of crime which had formerly been his own. He described that life as lacking any present influence, and found it strange how suddenly his "previous life's thinking pattern slid away from me." He had a sense of remoteness from this past, as if it had belonged to "another person."[27]

26. B. A. O. Williams, "Personal Identity and Individuation," in *Essays in Philosophical Psychology*, ed. Donald F. Gustafson (Garden City, N.Y.: Doubleday, 1964), pp. 325, 329.
27. *Autobiography of Malcolm X*, pp. 163, 170.

The fact that Malcolm X could remember the criminal activities of the "earlier self" corresponds to the sense in which, for Sartre, memories of past events remain objectively constant throughout the life of the body-subject. In this sense he is the same person he was earlier. But the fact that the earlier system of relations is experienced as discontinuous with the present system of interpreting events means that, in Sartre's second sense, he cannot be reidentified as the same person he was earlier. Malcolm Little's adoption of a new name, Malcolm X, was an appropriate and accurate response to the fact that he was a new person, in one sense.

Thus bodily identity, which was analyzed earlier as a necessary condition of personal identity, is not a sufficient condition, in this second sense of the term "person." Malcolm Little continued to be the same person he was at the time of h for as long as his (body-subject's) relations to people and to the objects of his world were organized in relation to E. When he adopted a new basic end, a new system of interpretation of objects and events—and new patterns of action as well as a new name—in accordance with that end, he became a new person. His actual remembering of events which occurred during his early life reflected this sense of discontinuity.

Sydney Shoemaker has argued that memory is one criterion of identity that we use with respect to other persons, but that it cannot be a criterion we use for ourselves. This is because we do not use any criteria at all in saying we remember doing so-and-so.[28] A rather interesting consequence of Sartre's analysis, I think, would be that memory could indeed be used by the person himself as a criterion of identity for himself *qua* system of relations.

Shoemaker has pointed out that, as things now stand, an action can be remembered from the inside only if it was my action, and that we cannot misidentify the subject of first-person memory claims. He imagines what it would be like if quasi remembering were possible; that is, if we could remember someone else's actions from the inside in the way we now remember our own actions. He imagines cases which will preserve the causal connection implicit in the previous awareness condition of remembering: people's bodies might undergo fission or fusion in such a way that both branches preserve the

28. Sydney S. Shoemaker, "Personal Identity and Memory," *Journal of Philosophy*, 56, no. 22 (October 1959): 873.

memories of the former single body, or two sets of memories are preserved in a single body.[29]

Sartre preserves the causal connection by the simpler assumption that the body-subject remains the same through time. But since Malcolm X can remember the actions of Malcolm Little from the inside, Sartre's analysis suggests that Malcolm must use interpretive remembering as a criterion for deciding whether an action was done by the earlier or by the present self. First-person memory claims may well be subject to the kind of error that would permit Malcolm X to confuse actions done by himself with actions done by Malcolm Little, particularly in cases where the remembered action was relatively neutral with respect to his fundamental goal, and where the memory itself was faint, contributing to the sense of "remoteness" of which he spoke.

In any case, since there could be more than one person (*qua* system of relations) per body, bodily identity cannot be a sufficient condition of personal identity in all senses of the term "person." Memory can be used as an additional criterion of personal identity by the person himself, as well as by others.

Sartre's idea of remembering as a form of intentional activity is in part an attempt to develop a concept which will fit the facts more closely than the theories of memory the Passivity form of psychological determinism would have to assume.

Sartre compared the remembered past to a "work of art" (*BN*, 500). To remember is to select certain properties of past events, to ignore others, and to organize the former properties in such a way as to make sense in terms of a present end, but an end which may radically alter. Since we are responsible for the end which shapes our remembering, the remembered past cannot be said to render us nonresponsible for present actions.

One of the best-known features of Sartre's thought has been his contention that human beings do not come "ready made" but that in one sense they create themselves.[30] There has been a tendency among English-speaking philosophers to dismiss this and other points made by Sartre as incredible or philosophically uninteresting. Sartre has contributed to this tendency by expressing himself, at times, more like a slogan writer than a

29. Sydney Shoemaker, "Persons and Their Pasts," *American Philosophical Quarterly*, 7, no. 4 (October 1970): 272, 279.
30. Sartre, "Existentialism Is a Humanism," p. 306.

philosopher. But I do not think Sartre can be dismissed quite so easily, and this discussion is an attempt to develop the creativity claim with respect to human memory. Sartre offered more than just a slogan about man's creativity. He has raised a set of new and philosophically interesting questions about memory and its relation to moral responsibility.

Since contemporary philosophers who espouse the Passivity View tend to appeal to evidence of the sort provided by such psychologists as B. F. Skinner, it seemed appropriate to examine the claims of Skinner, who says that his work supports the Passivity View. In the course of this examination it was found that Skinner is forced to give up one of the fundamental assumptions of the Passivity View (viz., that men are wholly passive with respect to prior and external events) when he discusses operant behavior. Skinner's resulting Activity View does not appear to support his nonresponsibility claim. Furthermore, it seems to be strikingly similar to Sartre's concept of a choosing, acting body-subject who develops, through time, a coherent set of relations to the world and to other people.

The major difference is that Skinner believes goals and purposes are determined by past experience, while Sartre believes human beings can "rupture with the given" in this important sense: they can imagine a state of affairs which does not and has never existed, and can act in such a way as to help bring that state of affairs into existence. The positing of such a goal is, for Sartre, the key to our creative structuring of past as well as present experience (*BN*, 478).

There is one way in which Sartre's claim that men (in one sense) create themselves can be connected in a more direct fashion with the Anglo-American philosophical tradition. Sartre's commentators have generally treated this claim as an ethical one, and Sartre himself sometimes does so. It seems to make more sense, however, to connect Sartre's creativity claim to questions that have been, and can be, raised in the philosophy of mind. Specifically, Sartre can be seen as offering a version of the bundle theory or logical construction view of persons; the "blank tablet" view of traditional empiricism is replaced by Sartre's "existence precedes essence."

Sartre believes that this theory has important implications for ethics, but the basic position he defends concerns the description to be given of human persons. This point can be clarified by turning to a discussion of character as a criterion of personal identity.

Chapter 4

Character and the Ambiguity of "I"

The person is, in addition to the body, a system of relations that the body-subject develops through time to objects and to other persons. Character is the past element of this system of relations, as known primarily by others; insofar as we are able to take a semi-spectator stance on ourselves in reflection, we can apply character predicates to ourselves (*BN*, 552). Sartre does not make a further distinction between character and, say, personality; he uses the terms "psyche," "ego," "self," as well as the term "character," to refer to the system of conscious relations (*BN*, 103, 162).

Earlier it was pointed out that one version of psychological determinism claims that external circumstances determine character and that character produces actions.[1] These two claims need to be distinguished. Sartre's answer to the view that external events determine character will be seen to have been given already, once we have discussed the second claim, that character produces action. Put in a somewhat different fashion, the question is whether the self which acts is to be distinguished from character so far formed, or whether these are the same?

Sartre's position, which is a form of Summary Theory, will be discussed in contrast with points made by Richard B. Brandt, C. A. Campbell, and P. H. Nowell-Smith, and in comparison with Stuart Hampshire's position. A claim that has been connected with the position that character produces actions is that actions are predictable from character descriptions.[2] Sartre denies this, but he says that actions are usually intelligible as being "in character." The latter point will be discussed in contrast with a few points made by Hume.

---

1. Cf. John Hospers, "What Means This Freedom?" in *Determinism and Freedom in the Age of Modern Science*, ed. Sidney Hook (New York: Collier Books, 1961), p. 131; Paul Edwards, "Hard and Soft Determinism," in ibid., p. 121.

2. Cf. P. H. Nowell-Smith, *Ethics* (London: Penguin Books, 1954), p. 279.

Character as the Pattern of Past Actions

Discussion can begin with the following question: Apart from the issue whether character is determined, should character be viewed as that which produces actions? Sartre claims that there are serious problems with this widely held position. Moral philosophers have frequently maintained that character stands in some kind of semi-causal relation to actions.[3] It is said that actions "grow out of . . . character,"[4] or actions are spoken of as "flowing from" character,[5] or it is said that "a person is blameworthy for an event only if it can be imputed to his character in the sense that it would not have happened had some defective trait been different,"[6] or it is claimed that "what I do will depend on my character."[7] Presumably, for each of these philosophers, it would be perfectly correct to use the locution "I ran away because I am a coward."

The kind of analysis Sartre would give of "I am a coward," however, would indicate that use of the above locution is a form of bad faith. For Sartre, it would be more correct to say "I am a coward because I ran away," since the use of the character-predicate is, in his view, a way of placing a series of past acts under a certain description. The question Sartre would want to pose is this: If we think of character as producing actions, then character is being thought of as something other than the acts themselves—and what is the nature of this "something more"? Is it, for instance, an entity or force that could exist wholly apart from *any* acts?

A clear statement of this claim is made by Richard B. Brandt, who says that even in the absence of knowing about particular actions, we may have an opinion of a person because of information about his character, and it is conceivable that we "could have good reason for thinking a man cowardly even if he had

3. It might seem to make more sense to speak of these relations as causal rather than semi-causal, except that many of those who claim that character produces action, or that actions can be explained by character, have doubted or denied that character is a cause. Powell has called attention to the strangeness of this denial, particularly since—for instance—neither Ryle nor Nowell-Smith allows for uncharacteristic actions. See Betty Powell, "Uncharacteristic Actions," *Mind*, 68 (1959): 494.

4. Hospers, "What Means This Freedom?" p. 131.

5. Edwards, "Hard and Soft Determinism," p. 119.

6. Richard B. Brandt, "Blameworthiness and Obligation," in *Essays in Moral Philosophy*, ed. A. I. Melden (Seattle: University of Washington Press, 1958), p. 31.

7. Nowell-Smith, *Ethics*, p. 287.

never acted so."[8] In a more recent article, Brandt makes clear that the kind of "something more" he has in mind is a persisting motive; he offers a dispositional analysis of character traits on the model of wants and aversions.[9] Brandt claims that personality tests might provide the kind of warrant needed to make judgments about character in the absence of actions of a given kind. He adds that Stuart Hampshire would find it impossible to think a man cowardly under such circumstances, since, for Hampshire, disposition statements mean a " 'summary of a trend' of past behavior and calculations."[10]

Sartre would agree, so far, with Hampshire. This is the central point, in fact, of his famous play *No Exit*. Garcin, who dreamed all his life of being a hero, behaved in a cowardly fashion when his big chance came; he tried to deny the relevance of his act by claiming that "a man is what he wills himself to be." His opponent, Inez, replies what Sartre would reply: "It's what one does, and nothing else, that shows the stuff one's made of." [11]

It has sometimes been assumed that a dispositional analysis must be given in terms of, or must include, subjunctive conditional statements. Brandt appears to make this assumption in the more recent of the two articles mentioned, where he discusses the Summary Theory as an alternative to, rather than as a form of, a dispositional view.[12] Brandt ignores Hampshire's insistence that statements concerning character and human dispositions are not necessarily hypothetical statements, although they may be.[13]

Sartre's Summary Theory of Character, like Hampshire's, is intended to give an analysis of dispositional properties (*BN*, 162; *TE*, 63, 70). Character traits are acquired, not intrinsic causal properties comparable to the solubility of sugar (*BN*, 162). Sartre acknowledges that we often think and speak of character traits by using hypothetical statements and that we often "assume a relation of causality" between a dispositional trait and its occurrences (*TE*, 63, 65). But he insists that these are risky procedures and may lead us to draw false inferences.

8. Brandt, "Blameworthiness and Obligation," p. 30.

9. Richard B. Brandt, "Traits of Character: A Conceptual Analysis," *American Philosophical Quarterly*, 7, no. 1 (January 1970): 23–37.

10. Brandt, "Blameworthiness and Obligation," p. 30, citing Stuart Hampshire, "Dispositions," *Analysis*, 14 (1953): 9.

11. Jean-Paul Sartre, *No Exit*, trans. Stuart Gilbert, in *No Exit and Three Other Plays* (New York: Random House, 1946), p. 44.

12. Brandt, "Traits of Character," p. 25.

13. Hampshire, "Dispositions," p. 10.

Sartre's position can be spelled out in the following way. For Sartre, the correct application of a character predicate to ourselves or to others means at least that (1) some actions have been performed which fit that description and (2) a sufficient number of such actions have been performed so that we can speak of "an organized unity of conduct patterns" (*BN*, 476).[14] Also that (3) within the time span being considered, no more than a few actions which might actively count against the character ascription have been performed. But need we mean more than this? Do we require, in addition, that character be something which can produce actions? The clearest way of presenting Sartre's answer is to show how he could analyze the phrase "I am a coward."

It was pointed out earlier that for both Sartre and Russell there is no need for an "I" in single thoughts (*TE*, 91).[15] The major function of the reflective use of "I," we recall, is to connect various acts of the body-subject. The "I" in "I am a coward" performs this function. That is to say, in Sartre's view, "I am a coward" might be translated, with no remainder, into some such series as this: "I ran from a lion at t_1," "I ran from a dog at t_2," "I ran from the war at t_3," ..., R_{t_n}. If these actions, $R_1, R_2, R_3, \ldots, R_n$, have occurred in my past, and if there are relatively few (or no) instances of brave acts in my past, it would be self-deception if I refuse to recognize these acts and, instead, attempt to claim unequivocally that I am not a coward (*BN*, 57).

But does this mean that it is therefore unequivocally true to say "I *am* a coward"? Sartre says that it is not. There would be nothing wrong with the assertion "I am a coward" if we were perfectly clear about the fact that in this case we are referring to a certain limited pattern of *past* actions which have been selected as the relevant actions from all of our other past actions, identified as instances of a certain kind, and unified under a certain description. In this case "the *I* is the ego as the unity of actions," an ideal unity which is the result of a synthetic unification (*TE*, 60, 76). It is a *"free unification,"* Sartre says, "for which substance was only a caricature" (*BN*, 561). In calling character or ego a "free unification," Sartre is claiming that the individual creates this pattern in time, act by act, in the way a melody is formed, note by note (*BN*, 468).

The mistake Sartre thinks is usually made, however, is to confuse this use of "I" with its use in referring to the subject

14. See also "Existentialism Is a Humanism," p. 301.
15. Cf. Russell, *Analysis of Mind*, p. 18.

which acts. It is thought that "I" must refer unequivocally to a substantial person, who possesses the essential characteristics of a car thief or coward, and who can be predicted to produce new actions consistent with his nature (*BN*, 58, 103, 561–62; *TE*, 81). A shift has been made, here, Sartre thinks, from the correct meaning of "I am a coward"—that is, as referring to the trend of five or twenty-five specific past actions—to an unwarranted hypostatic use of "I" to refer to the nature of a substantial agent.

As Sartre sees the problem, once the fatal shift in meaning has occurred, it is all too easy to believe, as we approach a new situation, that the die has been cast. The "I" whose body is now entering battle has been endowed with a substantial character from which will flow predictable actions: memories of R_1, R_2, R_3, . . . , R_n are awakened—fused together into an entity which is considered to be causally efficacious in producing a new act of cowardice.[16]

Sartre believes it is a form of bad faith to trade on the ambiguity of the word "I" in order to excuse one's cowardice, as in "I ran away because I am a coward." Even if acts R_1, R_2, R_3, . . . , R_n have occurred, it is not unequivocally true to say "I am a coward." It is not true *if* one thinks "I" here refers to an agent, and if one wishes to use this assertion in explanation of present actions or in prediction of future actions (*BN*, 64).[17]

The pattern of Sartre's argument, here as at certain earlier points, is to claim that "I" is ambiguous, and to claim, further-more, that this ambiguity can be accounted for without the need of invoking extra entities. It may make sense at this point to discuss more fully Sartre's claim that "I" is ambiguous, for this is certainly controversial.

The Ambiguity of "I"

Strawson claims that "I" is univocal. Sartre would certainly agree with Strawson that "I" is not equivocal in the Cartesian

16. A similar point is made by George Pitcher in his "Necessitarianism," *Philosophical Quarterly*, 2 (1961): 207–8. Pitcher, arguing against a neces-sitarian position, claims that to speak of a certain kind of character is only to say that one habitually does acts of a certain kind, and that therefore character cannot be conceived as the cause of the actions.

17. Sartre would agree with Stuart Hampshire's point that when we

sense of referring to a body-substance and a person-substance. Strawson considers only one other alternative. He appears to think that unless "I" were univocal in referring to the person who possesses both physical and conscious attributes, then experiences would be ownerless.[18] Since Sartre does not claim that experiences are "ownerless," but regards the human body as the subject of experiences as well as the possessor of physical characteristics, why doesn't Sartre just say that "I" refers univocally to the human body-subject?

It was mentioned earlier that, for Sartre, one use of "I" is to refer to the body. One difficulty that Strawson faces in claiming "I" refers univocally to the person, and in claiming also that it is conceivable that the person could change to another body, is obvious if we try to take the person, rather than the body, as the subject of such statements as "I am six feet tall." For suppose the six-foot person tries to change into a new five-foot body? It is not only the person's tailor who is going to have difficulty with this situation. The point Sartre can make here is that in many cases "I" really refers quite strictly to the body, and could not refer to a person who possesses material attributes and could conceivably change bodies. In this case the "I" refers to the body *qua* physical object; "I" can also refer to the body *qua* conscious subject, as in "I see the tree."

But there are at least two nonbodily uses of the word "I" for Sartre. In one passage Strawson says that the no-ownership theorist thinks the nonbodily use of "I" "does not refer at all."[19] Earlier, in discussing Wittgenstein, he said that for the no-ownership theorist, the nonbodily use of "I" "*does not denote a possessor.*"[20] Sartre could point out that these are not equivalent claims; he does not deny that the nonbodily uses of "I" make a reference, but he maintains that they do not denote a possessor. One of the nonbodily uses of "I," to refer to character, has just been described. For Sartre, the most important application of this use of "I" is to our moral discourse. Here we definitely want to talk about something other than the physical characteristics of the body, such as its being six feet

---

write a character testimonial, we are not making a prediction, although this might provide grounds for a prediction. Hampshire says that if the prediction turns out to be false, it does not follow that the character description was false, since these are "summarising statements" rather than hypothetical statements of the form appropriate for descriptions of causal properties. Hampshire, "Dispositions," pp. 7–8.

18. Strawson, *Individuals,* p. 99.
19. Ibid.
20. Ibid., p. 90, n. 2.

tall, and also wish to speak of something other than particular acts of the conscious body-subject. We use "I" when we want to speak of certain characteristic patterns of action, as in "I am a thief" or "I am an irascible person." Some kinds of action series are particularly important when we wish to make moral evaluations, and it is in this connection that Sartre would insist on the distinction between different uses of "I."

There is at least one other morally important nonbodily use of "I," according to Sartre, which will be discussed in the next chapter. This use refers to the self I am trying to be. It is exhibited in its clearest form in such statements as "I am a Christian," when there are no past actions to refer to in support of the claim. Sartre's famous analysis of bad faith can be interpreted as resting on the claim that people mistake one use of "I" for another, or that they use it to refer univocally to a person-substance without making any distinction between its several uses (*BN*, 66—67).[21]

It should be very clear that the "I" which sometimes refers to the body-subject cannot be univocal. The body is born and dies on specific dates, although there may be some need to decide whether a one-month embryo counts as a live human body and whether a man is alive when some (but not all) of his vital functions have ceased. A pattern of action usually has a much less specific beginning, although it may end quite abruptly. These patterns do not begin on the date of physical birth. A child may steal only an occasional toy for a long period; but if he is more likely *not* to do this, we would certainly not speak of an existing pattern of action. If, a few years later, he began to steal habitually, an observer might see the beginnings of this

---

21. There are other ways of reading the ambiguity which underlies Sartre's analysis of bad faith. On p. 29 of his unpublished paper "Sartre's Account of Self-Deception," Frithjof H. Bergmann sees the ambiguity not in the word "I" but in the moral predicates. See also Arne Naess, *Four Modern Philosophers* pp. 316—18. Naess thinks the ambiguity is in the word "is," in such Sartrean dicta as "*for-itself* is defined . . . as being what it is not and not being what it is" (*BN*, p. lxv). A less sympathetic critic has simply said that Sartre meant that consciousness is a contradiction (William Earle, "Man as the Impossibility of God," in *Christianity and Existentialism: Essays by Wm. Earle, James M. Edie and John Wild* [Evanston, Ill.: Northwestern University Press, 1963], p. 107).

Sartre's distinction between different uses of "I" can be combined with earlier points to form the suggestion that there is need for a special logic of consciousness. Sartre hints at such a need when he says that the law of identity is synthetic, not analytic, because it is valid for only one form of existence, things, and not for the other basic form of existence, consciousness (*BN*, p. 58). A. J. Ayer comments on Sartre's originality with respect to this point in "Novelist-Philosophers," p. 13.

pattern of action during the early period. Such a person may in one sense truly say of himself "I am a thief" when the pattern is firmly established, but if he should reform and become an honest man, the "I" who was a thief no longer exists, even though the "I" which is the body-subject persists. "I" cannot, then, refer univocally to the body-subject.

Strawson examines only two possible nonbodily uses of the word "I": the Cartesian and the no-ownership doctrine. The discussion of Sartre's position makes clear that Strawson's list of possibilities is not exhaustive. Against both the Cartesian view and the no-ownership doctrine, as he has explained it, Strawson argues that consciousness and corporeal characteristics can be ascribed to the very same thing.[22] Sartre does not disagree with this point; the disagreement lies rather in what both types of characteristic should be ascribed to. Strawson claims that this must be the person; Sartre claims that the human body can be the subject of conscious relations as well as possessor of physical properties. The point of maintaining the nonbodily uses of "I," for Sartre, is not for either of the reasons suggested by Strawson. Sartre does not want to use "I" either to refer to an immaterial thinking substance or to deny that there is a subject of experiences. For Sartre, the important nonbodily uses of "I" are connected with our moral discourse.

Sartre has suggested an analysis of character dispositions so that the self which acts (body-subject) is distinguished from character so far formed (patterns of past actions.) Character, so conceived, does not produce actions since it is nothing more than past acts themselves under a certain description. There is no need for an extra force or entity (character) which could exist apart from all acts, as in Brandt's position, and which could be conceived as the producer of new acts.

Applying Character Predicates

In addition to the point that there is no need for an extra entity in order to account for the distinction between the agent and his character, Sartre appeals to ordinary practices of applying character predicates in support of his claim that character could

22. Strawson, *Individuals*, p. 93.

not be something wholly apart from past acts. It was noted that Brandt says character traits, conceived as persisting motives, might exist in the absence of any actions of the suitable type, and that good reason for their existence might be found in psychological tests.

Sartre could point out that ordinary practices support his view that we can say Jones has a character trait of a given sort only if Jones has exhibited actions of the relevant kind. Brandt's example can be changed slightly to show one difficulty. If it were correct to say that Jones is a coward even though he has never behaved in a cowardly fashion, then by the same token it ought to be all right to say that Smith is honest, even though *he* has never behaved so. But, in our ordinary practice of recommending others, it would be very misleading to make such claims. The underlying assumption appears to be that the application of character predicates is a kind of recognition of achievement or failure in acquiring some particular kind of habitual activity.

In the absence of some recognizable achievement, we do not praise others by giving them good character references. In the absence of some observable instances of someone's failing to meet a standard, it is likely that he might sue for libel if we say he is dishonest or a coward. Brandt, of course, does not claim that we will say a man is a coward, only that we will think it; but his claim is that we can think it with good reason. Sartre would deny that there could be any good reason in such a case, since the man would simply not have acquired a given character trait in the absence of opportunities to act in a given manner.

Sartre's most concerted attack on this question, however, is not centered on the kind of situation in which we make statements about someone else's character, but on situations when we apply character predicates to ourselves. If it were correct for me to speak of Johnson as having an honest character, even though he had not behaved so, surely I may speak of myself as honest or brave even though I have not acted honestly or bravely. But we simply do not accept such statements. Sartre speaks of bad faith when I claim to have a character trait in the absence of having performed a series of actions of that kind, as Garcin did. Sartre also speaks of bad faith when I deny having a character of the kind that my past actions proclaim (*BN*, 57, 63). Such persons are deceiving themselves, we would usually agree, or they are trying to deceive others, or perhaps they are boasting when they make such claims. But we do *not* say that they are honest or brave. Yet if character were something entirely other than actions performed, on what grounds would we condemn such utterances?

According to Brandt, we might accept Garcin's claim that he is truly a brave man provided certain psychological tests showed that he had, as he claimed he has, a persisting motivation to be courageous. But wouldn't this, rather, be a reason for questioning whether the tests really measured what they purport to measure? Sartre could point out that if no behavior has occurred, presumably the character tests in question would need to rely heavily on the agent's own utterances. But this procedure seems dubious, for Garcin would surely have given answers appropriate to his image of what he wanted to be—a courageous man. (In terms of Sartre's analysis, Garcin confused two uses of "I"—its use to refer to a series of past actions and its use to refer to the ideal self.) This will not do, however, because the label "courageous man" must be won, it cannot simply be wanted.

Even if the motive to be a brave man is thought to be a very strong force (which Sartre denies), it alone is not sufficient to warrant the correct application of the character predicate. Character traits, unlike intrinsic causal properties (e.g., the solubility of sugar in water), must be acquired. They are acquired, as Aristotle pointed out, by performing acts of the kind in question.[23]

Uncharacteristic Acts

If one thinks of character traits as causal or semi-causal dispositional properties, it may be appropriate to give the meaning or

---

23. Sartre explicitly compares his notion of character with the Greek view of *hexis* (*BN*, p. 162). Professor Gary Cox has noted that a problem with my interpretation of Sartre is that the notion of *hexis* includes the notion that character causes action. I think Professor Cox is correct in calling attention to a difficulty here. Sartre's point might have been clearer if he had spelled out exactly what he understood by the concept of *hexis*. In an early passage in *Being and Nothingness* he denies that there is *hexis* behind the act (p. xlvi). He makes it abundantly clear, whenever he discusses the concept of action, that neither character nor motives (conceived as existent forces) can be causes of actions (see, e.g., *BN*, pp. 437–38). For this reason it seemed most likely that, in speaking of his own view as a form of *hexis*, Sartre meant to accept that part of the Aristotelian view which affirms that character is a disposition acquired through the performing of actions, but to reject the additional idea, usually included in the notion of *hexis*, that character produces actions.

part of the meaning of the character predicate in hypothetical terms: "If one were to place X in dangerous circumstances, he would . . . " It would, then, also make sense to explain our present action by reference to the character trait.

Sartre, who denies that character produces actions, does not deny that there is an implicit future reference in such cases. It is not a prediction based on causal grounds, however, but a choice of future end that is involved (*TE*, 63–65). The attempt to excuse ourselves with the alleged explanation "I ran away because I am a coward" is really to make a present reference to a number of past actions in terms of a choice of a future end. In this case the choice is to continue being a coward. In the light of this choice, we sometimes experience our character (that is, series of past acts) as exerting a compelling force over our present act, as in habits that are difficult to break (*BN*, 501–4, 474–75).[24]

We can most clearly know, on those occasions when an action is out of character, that our character (*qua* series of past acts) does not explain or produce our present acts. This point can be developed in the form of a reply to Brandt's argument purporting to show that "the Summary Theory is simply wrong." Brandt argues that we often make inferences about an individual's character traits "on the basis of a *single* piece of behavior."[25] We could not confidently make such inferences if to apply a character predicate were simply to assert that the individual in question had acted in a particular manner in the past. He gives the example of a boy who refuses to do a certain thing even under the threat of being beaten by older boys. Thus the single instance is sufficient evidence for a justified inference that the boy is courageous, Brandt claims, and therefore the Summary Theory is wrong.

Sartre could reply to Brandt that while the inference based on a single instance may be *correct*, it is not justified. It may turn out to be correct if additional past instances can be adduced; if no past instances are found but if subsequent actions also exhibit a pattern of courage, then one may look back at this single instance as the first in a series of actions. But the inference is not *justified* in the single instance. Sartre can

24. This last point is somewhat interesting since it means that Sartre is not only not appealing to introspection as the support for his claims but maintaining that introspection can give us false clues (*TE*, pp. 64, 65; *BN*, p. 471). This is one respect, as we will see, in which Sartre's position differs quite sharply from that of C. A. Campbell. This may also be a point of difference from the orthodox phenomenological viewpoint.

25. Brandt, "Traits of Character," p. 26.

point out that there are several alternatives, and that the inference to the boy's courage may not even be correct. It may have been a single out-of-character action, for usually he runs away. It may have been an act which signals a radical conversion to a new character structure: he used to run away, but he won't anymore.

Again, it may be that as one examines the boy's past actions it becomes clear that the single instance may have been misdescribed. To be sure, he has never behaved courageously before, which is why Brandt calls it a single instance. But he has repeatedly showed himself to be stubborn, and the instance is simply a new action in a series of stubborn actions. Or, again, maybe he is a coward in the sense that he is even more afraid of eternal hellfire, which he believes would result from doing the thing in question, than he is of being beaten. (The fact that the single piece of behavior can be considered under more than one description, however, gives rise to other problems, which will be discussed in the next chapter.)

Still again, in the case of certain kinds of actions, an old character structure seems to disintegrate; a good man goes berserk and kills his family, for example.

In none of these cases would the inference to a character trait, based on a single instance, have been justified. Since one could discover whether he is correct only by knowing patterns of past action, Brandt seems to be mistaken in his claim that inference is justified in the single instance.

In most of the counterexamples offered there is no way we could say that the individual's previous character had produced the uncharacteristic action or the new series of actions. Brandt does not discuss the problem of uncharacteristic actions in relation to his own analysis of character traits. However, others who agree with Brandt in claiming that character produces actions have discussed the question of uncharacteristic actions. Nowell-Smith, for instance, suggests the following move against C. A. Campbell's suggestion that a free action is one that is not predictable from knowing the character of the agent: simply deny that the uncharacteristic action is the action of the person.[26] This move can be pursued briefly in order to compare a few points in Sartre's position with some corresponding points in Campbell's position.

Sartre shares with Campbell the view that the self which acts and decides is to be sharply distinguished from character so far

---

26. Nowell-Smith, *Ethics*, pp. 282–83.

formed. Character is viewed by both as a creation or accomplishment, not as the producer of actions.[27] Campbell, who supports his position by an appeal to introspection, has been criticized for this method.[28] Sartre bases his distinction between the agent and his character, at this point, on the fact that many actions are not consistent with previous character structure, and some may be radically opposed to it. Another difference between Sartre and Campbell is in the nature of the agent-self; it is this difference that permits Sartre to answer Nowell-Smith's criticism of Campbell's position, and in a way that Campbell perhaps could not. For Campbell, the "self is a spiritual substance."[29] For Sartre, however, it is the body-subject which produces actions, thinks, and makes moral and other decisions.

Nowell-Smith, as we saw, suggests that an action which is not predictable from the agent's character is not his action at all. He proceeds to argue that the only thing we could say, if such a case ever happened, is that it happened by chance or by Divine Grace. He points out that Campbell would attempt to distinguish indeterminism from self-determinism. The problem, Nowell-Smith remarks, is that self-determinism either means " 'determined by *his* motives and character,' as opposed to 'forced on him by circumstances or other people,' " which Campbell rejects, or " 'determined by the self.' " The latter won't work, however, because it is necessary, for the purposes of ascribing responsibility and punishing people, to have a criterion for deciding whether the self which did the action is the same as the self to be held responsible.[30]

Sartre's distinction between the body-subject, which acts, and character, which is the past pattern of such acts, does not prevent him from providing such criteria of identity. It is the person *qua* body-subject that we now hold in prison and propose to punish; it is the presence of the same body-subject at the scene of the crime that we propose to establish via eyewitness accounts, fingerprints, photographs, etc. We can question the body-subject about memories of the night of the crime, and—to the extent that these corroborate what is known about

27. C. A. Campbell, "In Defence of Free Will," in *In Defence of Free Will, with Other Philosophical Essays* (London: Allen & Unwin, 1967), pp. 43–44.

28. E.g., Nowell-Smith, *Ethics*, pp. 280–81.

29. C. A. Campbell, *On Selfhood and Godhood* (London: Allen & Unwin, 1957; New York: Macmillan, 1957), p. 92.

30. Nowell-Smith, *Ethics*, pp. 282–83.

the body's whereabouts—they can be accepted as a genuine, although secondary, criterion of identity. It is possible in Sartre's view, in other words, to provide a very clear sense in which we say an action is y's action, for purposes of holding y responsible, even though the action in question is an out-of-character action. It is not only possible for Sartre to handle this type of case in this way, this is the way we actually handle such cases.

Nowell-Smith says that using bodily identity as the primary criterion of personal identity is a "rather crude course." [31] Crude it may be, but it is difficult to see any other way of doing things. If we really believe that character produces actions, and that character is to be used as the primary criterion of personal identity, then what we ought to do, when a crime is committed, is draw up a description of the character of a man who could have been predicted to have committed just such an action and distribute this character description to law enforcement agencies, instead of wasting time with fingerprints. What happens if one hundred men with such a character are discovered? Hanging all of them might be one way of handling the problem, but it is not our way. Character descriptions can fit a large number of people, but we have a rather stubborn belief that just one of these people committed this crime.

If character is our primary criterion of personal identity, how can we distinguish between the doer of the deed and those who might have done the deed? Unfortunately, we can distinguish them only by our crude method of establishing bodily presence at the scene of the crime, or bodily presence at some definite place when a third party was paid to commit the murder.

Another procedure that we do *not* follow is releasing a man, when we have conclusive physical evidence of his guilt, simply on the ground that his murder was out of character and therefore was not his action. We do not assume that Divine Grace or chance intervened, and despite Nowell-Smith, such cases occur. The fact that a crime was out of character, or that it occurred preceding or following a change of character, definitely makes a difference in our handling of his case, however. We tend to look for extenuating circumstances in such cases. Sartre does not have to deny that character is a relevant criterion of personal identity in our reward and punishment procedures; he only denies that it is the fundamental criterion of identity. If a hardened murderer undergoes a radical transformation and be-

31. Ibid., p. 283.

comes a good man, Sartre insists that in one sense he *is* a new person. This is recognized in parole procedures. What is recognized, however, is not that a new agent has suddenly appeared on the scene but that the same agent (Jones *qua* body-subject) has developed a completely new system of relations to the world and to other people. His new character is a series of new acts viewed as tending toward a new type of end. It is not that which produces the new series.

If there is good reason to think that when we speak of a character trait we are referring, as Sartre claims, to nothing less and nothing more than a series of past actions placed under a certain description, then the other question, with which we began—whether past events determine character—can be seen as already answered. What is probably being asked, in this case, is whether each particular past action was wholly determined by prior and external events. For if the agent's past choice of acts were considered to be one of the significant causes of his resulting character, there would be no apparent reason to deny that his present choice of action is a significant cause of his continuing or changing character. Each action occurs at a different time. At any given time, when faced with the need to act, we view the given circumstances as an instrumental complex, selecting certain aspects of our remembered past as meaningful within the same framework of interpretation. Our remembered past may include a series of our own acts similar to an act we now choose to perform, if our fundamental end has not changed. We may, however, choose a new fundamental project; in the light of a new end, our acts from now on will be discontinuous with the past series of actions, which constitute our character until now. Character is not a force or a substance; its description cannot provide a guaranteed prediction about future actions.

The Relative Coherence of Character

It should be pointed out that Sartre holds that others' actions are not exactly predictable even when an action series has not been discontinued (*BN*, 400). We cannot predict in detail what others will do, even if their actions are "in character," he claims. Others' actions, in other words, do not appear mechanical to us. On the other hand, their actions are comprehensible to us; that is, they form patterns. It may be this fact that has led many philosophers to believe that character produces actions. We are rarely (although occasionally) wholly surprised by what others do. The two errors Sartre tries to avoid are thinking that character is a substance or force with definite causal properties and thinking that there is no coherence in human thinking and action.

The latter aspect of Sartre's position can be developed by comparing what he has to say with some points made by the bundle theorists. Hume rejected an immaterial person-substance on the basis of our inability to experience such a substance. Sartre, as we saw, agrees that there is no experience of an immaterial subject, but it is not for this reason that he denies it exists, for even if there were such an entity, it would lead to an infinite regress if we supposed we could experience it. Instead, Sartre gave arguments to show there is no need for an extra entity, an immaterial person-substance. Sartre would agree with Hume, however, in saying that when we reflect we are aware of a succession of acts. Sartre adds that we connect thinkings, desirings, and performings when we use the term "I," and it is to this synthetic construct that we refer when we speak of ego or character.

One difficulty shows up in Hume's assertion that each man is "nothing but a bundle or collection of different perceptions, which succeed each other with an inconceivable rapidity and are in a perpetual flux and movement."[32]   The standard objection to this and similar passages is that Hume begs the question. Hume has presupposed a perceiver, in the very passage in which he denies that there is a subject of perceptions. Sartre does not accuse Hume of begging the question, but his own account of the body-subject, and his analysis of the structures of reflective and prereflective consciousness, can be seen as ways of resolving the standard difficulty faced by the bundle theorists.

However, the objection Sartre makes to Hume's claim is that "man is a totality and not a collection" (*BN*, 568). In other words, Hume has performed a real service in attacking the concept of an immaterial subject, but his discussion completely fails to explain why an individual's actions are usually intelligible as being "in character" even though those actions are not predictable in detail (*BN*, 400, 481, 561).

It was argued earlier that the philosopher who believes that character produces acts would have difficulty in accounting for

---

32. David Hume, *A Treatise of Human Nature*, ed. L. A. Selby-Bigge (Oxford: Clarendon Press, 1888), bk. I, pt. IV, sec. VI, p. 252.

uncharacteristic acts or for the first act which signals a radical conversion. Hume's problem would be different. He could look for some kind of external precipitating factor to explain an uncharacteristic act or a radical conversion, but his particular difficulty would be to explain the relatively high degree of coherence before and after a conversion or an uncharacteristic act. Unless there had been some pattern of action, how could we have described a man as cowardly? Hume is to some extent aware of the difficulty, and suggests, as some later bundle theorists were also to suggest, that memory provides the link between successive perceptions.[33]

In his discussion of the associationist memory model, Sartre suggests one reason why memory alone would not be sufficient to provide the kind of link Hume seeks. The organized nature of memory must be explained in terms of something other than memory itself, since those external stimuli which could call forth similar memories appear only chaotically.[34] To use an analogy, the Humean model would merely produce a sequence of sounds, without any melodic or rhythmic patterns. It is clear that Hume is dissatisfied with his own solution, for in the *Appendix* he confesses that, having rejected the theory that there is a self or substance, he has been unable to "explain the principles, that unite our successive perceptions in our thought or consciousness."[35]

Sartre does not accept the logical constructionist or bundle theory of the self as a total account of the concept of a person. He appears to defend a version of the logical constructionist position, however, with respect to that nonbodily sense of "I" which refers to character. Anthony Quinton has defended a version of the bundle theory which adds continuity of character to memory as a criterion of "soul" identity.[36] Sartre would probably be sympathetic to Quinton's addition, for this would come much closer to suggesting the kind and degree of internal coherence among the various acts to be connected, which Sartre thought Hume failed to provide. Quinton's addition of continuity of character permits him to distinguish, as Sartre also wished to do, between earlier and later selves.

Sartre would wish to take a few additional steps, however.

33. Ibid., p. 261. See also H. P. Grice, "Personal Identity," *Mind*, 50 (1941): 340.
34. Sartre, *Imagination*, pp. 49–56, 111–13.
35. Hume, *A Treatise of Human Nature*, p. 636.
36. Anthony Quinton, "The Soul," *Journal of Philosophy*, 59, no. 15 (July 1962): 398.

Since he has given a summary view of character, the body which has performed the series of acts which constitute character is itself one of the fundamental links in the system.[37]

Furthermore, since character is not an existing force or an entity, one must still ask what connects the various acts which make up an early self or character and what connects the various acts which constitute a later self or character of the same body.

Sartre, having rejected the idea that the ego or character is an immaterial substance, says that this unity can be partially explained by the fact that individuals are dissatisfied by the lack of a substantial character or ego. Each individual body-subject, disturbed by the potential chaos and ephemerality implicit in the recognition that there is no substantial ego, chooses an ideal self, or fundamental project of being, which will have the "characteristics of identity, of purity, of permanence" which the substantial ego would possess if there were such a thing (*BN*, 93).

It is by reference to this ideal self, the future "I," that we organize memories of past events; it is also by reference to the ideal self that we choose present actions. The intelligibility of an individual's characteristic actions and ideas, as well as their unpredictability in detail, can be explained by the fact that he makes a long-term choice of the self he is trying to be, but has to invent the ways of trying to become that self from one situation to the next. The ideal self, or fundamental project of being, can be considered a fourth criterion of personal identity in Sartre's theory.

37. Russell made the suggestion, also, that a person is constituted by the "relations of the thoughts to each other and to the body." *The Analysis of Mind*, p. 18.

Chapter 5

A New Criterion of Personal Identity: The Fundamental Project

Sartre thinks we can find the "individual person in the initial project which constitutes him" (*BN*, 563). In this chapter the fundamental project will be discussed in its role as one of the fundamental links which connect conscious relations. It will be shown how the notion of the fundamental project plays a key role in Sartre's theories of rationality and freedom. Finally, Sartre's concept of choice will be contrasted with Aristotle's, and a comparison will be made between Sartre's concept of a choice of fundamental project and Aristotle's suggestion that there should be a life plan.

The Fundamental Project as Relation of Co-personality

It was suggested that that part of Sartre's concept of a person which deals with a system of conscious relations could be considered as a version of the logical construction view of persons. Sartre shares with other logical constructionists the belief that there is no immaterial self-substance. The central problem faced by the logical constructionist is that if there is no spiritual substance to which various experiences belong, he must account in some other way for the fact that your experiences all belong to you and mine all belong to me. What links my experiences, if there are no person-substances? It was suggested that part of Sartre's answer is that the body-subject is what has, and therefore links, experiences. But this could not be the whole answer, since there could be more than one system of conscious relations for the same continuing body.

The logical constructionists have tried to find a psychological, rather than a physical, link. As Shoemaker points out, the answer they most commonly give is that memory is the relation of "co-personality" that connects a single individual's experiences.[1] Sartre could agree with one of the standard objections to this proposal. Butler, commenting on Locke's version of the claim that memory makes personal identity, points out that Locke's claim implies either that he can remember every moment of his existence and everything he has done or that selfhood has gaps in it. However, says Butler, it is obvious that "consciousness of personal identity presupposes, and therefore cannot constitute, personal identity."[2]

Sartre could agree with the latter point. Memory could not itself be the primary relation of co-personality that links a person's experience. In the objective sense of remembering, in which everything I remember is something witnessed or experienced by this body, there would be no way of making a distinction between really remembering and seeming to remember something without reference to the body's presence at the scene in question.[3] In this sense, then, memory as a criterion of personal identity is secondary, or presupposes bodily identity.

But neither could interpretive memory be the primary relation of co-personality which links the elements of the system of conscious relations. According to Sartre, we have to explain the rather perplexing fact that memory itself occurs within a system of interpretation. Sartre argued, as we saw, that Hume's account of the mind as a collection of perceptions would not permit Hume to explain the degree of coherence which is actually discoverable in individuals' conscious relations to the world. Our remembering is organized; we selectively forget and remember. Something other than memory itself must be brought into the picture, if we are going to account for the way memory links us to certain properties of past events. Thus in the nonobjective sense also, memory as a criterion of personal identity is secondary. Sartre claimed that interpretive remembering pre-

1. Shoemaker, *Self-Knowledge and Self-Identity*, p. 151. Shoemaker suggests that it was probably Hume's theory of memory that led Hume to suggest that a person's successive "perceptions" are held together by the relations of cause and effect and resemblance.

2. Joseph Butler, "On Personal Identity," in *Body, Mind, and Death*, ed. Antony Flew, Problems of Philosophy Series (New York: Macmillan, 1964; London: Collier-Macmillan, 1964), p. 167.

3. Shoemaker makes a similar point in his *Self-Knowledge and Self-Identity*, p. 200.

supposes a continuity of the fundamental project which organizes the system of interpretation within which events are selectively remembered.

Sartre's account of memory would permit him to answer the following objection, made by Shoemaker, to the idea that there could be a discoverable relationship of co-personality within a logical constructionist view. Shoemaker argues that one could establish empirically that a memory stands in the relation R to a present experience only if one could also theoretically establish that it does not stand in R to that present experience. But if one could find that a remembered experience does not stand in R to my present experience, and if R were the relation of co-personality, "then I could find that an experience I remember was not my experience."[4] Shoemaker denies that this is theoretically possible.

Sartre would reply that, in the sense of "my" with which we are now concerned, it is possible to remember an experience that is not my experience. He laid the groundwork for this point when he distinguished between an objective and non-objective element of remembering. In the sense in which I am a body-subject, everything I remember was my experience. But we are concerned now with the person *qua* system of relations or logical construct. Sartre pointed out that we can remember a past event as either continuous with or discontinuous with the present system. Malcolm X, we recall, remembered his previous life of crime as if it had been the life of another person; and Sartre could account for this by pointing out that the body-subject remained the same during a period when the person *qua* system of relations had been replaced by a new system.

Sartre can maintain, then, that in one sense there is a discoverable relationship of co-personality. He has rejected, however, the usual answer to the question of what holds the person, *qua* construct, together. Sartre agrees with the logical constructionists in rejecting an immaterial substance as a persisting entity. In addition, he would reject their usual answer, that memory is the primary relation of co-personality. He does not claim that memory is irrelevant, but only that it is a secondary criterion of identity. In the objective sense, memory is dependent on bodily identity. In the interpretive sense, memory is dependent on the continuity of a fundamental project which organizes the system of conscious relations.

4. Ibid., p. 149.

Other answers that Sartre could be seen to have rejected are, first, that character is an entity which persists in time. Sartre points out that character can change abruptly, and that some account must be given of what ordinarily unites it. Again, he has rejected a possible answer that consciousness is a kind of container that could keep experiences collected in one mental space—a solution Hume may have toyed with in his theater example.[5] One way of putting Sartre's answer to the question of what unites the person *qua* system of relations is *nothing*.

This answer has already been given, in a number of ways, throughout this work. Sartre does not deny that there is coherence in the system of relations; that is not his point at all. His point, rather, is that human beings can be intentionally related to nonexisting states of affairs and objects. It is by reference to a particular nonexisting state of affairs, an ideal self or fundamental project, that the body-subject organizes its thoughts and actions through time. It is by reference to this particular nonthing, this future end, that the body-subject perceives objects within an instrumental framework. It is by reference to the fundamental project that we select certain properties of past events to remember, and by reference to the same project or ideal self that we interpret those properties. The ideal self is what gives a coherent pattern to our actions; if we choose another project, that character pattern is replaced by a new one.

The fundamental project is the relation of co-personality, or a unifying link between experiences, insofar as the person is a system of conscious relations to the world and to other people (*BN*, 561). Some of Sartre's semi-humorous claims about "nothing" might be less startling if he were interpreted as calling attention to what he sees as the very puzzling fact—that what unites the person *qua* construct is a nonexistent state of affairs. For example, he says "negation is the cement which realizes this unity" (*BN*, 21). Again, this interpretation makes sense of Sartre's suggestion that "I" can refer ambiguously to character or past acts and to a future self: "it is not what it is (past) and it is what it is not (future)" (*BN*, 123).

5. *BN*, pp. 313–14. Sartre's objections to the notion of consciousness as a mental space (a "closed box") do not apply to the notion of a brain, which occupies physical space. Sartre expresses sympathy for a conception of the brain as a performer of syntheses. He cites physiological research performed at the turn of this century in support of this conception of the brain. Sartre suggests that this conception replaced an earlier physiological theory of "cerebral localization" which had tended to support the atomistic associationist account of consciousness and its functions. *Imagination*, pp. 65–66.

Rationality and the Fundamental Project

Sartre rejected the Humean position which in effect made the person a disconnected collection of "perceptions." Instead, he argued, the person is a pattern or "ensemble" of acts. The body-subject creates a self, a system of conscious relations to the world, by reference to a connecting link: the ideal self or fundamental project. In this sense, Sartre may be seen as providing a new interpretation of the ancient idea that man is distinguished from things in nature by his rationality.

Sartre's view of rationality, however, is quite different from the familiar one that connects rationality with universalizability. In *Thought and Action* Stuart Hampshire makes explicit a theory of rationality that is like the one implicit in Sartre's remarks on the fundamental project. Hampshire presents his own view, not Sartre's, when he says that rationality is nothing more than the opposite of disconnectedness, and that connectedness requires a "trajectory of intention" within which behavior sequences can be seen to fit into an intelligible whole— intelligible, that is, in the sense of being directed toward an end.[6]

Sartre clearly rejects the idea that particular acts of the individual are irrational or absurd. It is not only the case that each action has some point to it, but that there is some underlying point which connects our actions with each other. This is true of our emotionally charged, as well as our calmer, acts and responses. Sartre does not treat emotions as unintelligible responses. Rather, emotions are part of that total organization of responses to a world which is structured in the light of our fundamental project. To react emotionally is to deal ineffectively with that world; thus our anger is a response to the critic we cannot answer effectively. But the emotional reaction makes sense in the light of our goal.[7]

Particular acts, then, emotional or otherwise, can be understood in terms of the individual's choice of a fundamental project (*BN*, 437, 452–53). This is important because there has been a great deal of popular emphasis on the alleged absurdity or irrationality of outlook of the existentialist position. It is only on the level of the choice of a fundamental project, the unifying principle of the whole system of relations the individ-

6. Hampshire, *Thought and Action*, pp. 144, 146, 149.
7. Sartre, *The Emotions: Outline of a Theory*, trans. Bernard Frechtman (New York: Wisdom Library, 1948), pp. 18, 58.

ual has with the world, that Sartre speaks of an absurd or unjustifiable choice (*BN*, 464). (We will look in a moment at what he means by "choice.") Sartre's point is not that reasons are generally irrelevant to decision making, or that reason should be rejected in favor of, say, impulse, but rather that what counts as a reason must be decided upon before one can begin the process of decision making on the level of particular acts (*BN*, 444–46).

If one has already chosen, as one's fundamental project, to try to be a good Catholic, then "the Pope said so" counts as a strong reason. It does not count at all as a reason for an atheist, a Protestant, a Jew, or for anyone else whose fundamental project does not include the Roman Catholic system of ideas. More basically, it cannot count as a reason in favor of deciding to adopt the project of becoming a Catholic. The choice of fundamental project is in part a decision on what will count as reasons for us (*BN*, 461–62).

Such an approach to reason-giving might lead to universalizable principles if the assumption were made that there are basic nonbiological ends common to all men. Sartre denies this assumption.[8] As examples of fundamental projects he has included such uncommon ones as willing oneself to be inferior, or being a thief (*BN*, 471).[9] It is not at all clear that many considerations might count as common reasons, given a nearly limitless variety of fundamental ends possible for human beings.

It does not appear that Sartre's account of reason-giving could be easily countered by claiming there are ends common to all men. If this were intended as an empirical claim, it seems to be false. If it were intended as a prescription, however, of the form "all men should have common ends," one is at a loss to know what kind of reasons could be given that would convince someone who believes that variety is the spice of life. The

---

8. This is one of the few points I disagree with in Joseph Fell's lucid article, "Sartre's Theory of Motivation: Some Clarifications." *Journal of the British Society for Phenomenology*, 1, no. 2 (May 1970): 30. Fell interprets Sartre as saying there is only one ultimate goal for all human behavior, namely, the desire to be God, or, what amounts to the same, the desire to be conscious substance (integral, permanent, independent).

Certainly Sartre does speak this way at times. One must ask, however, whether he really is stating a common goal, given that it is a totally unspecified project, or whether he intends to state the common criteria by which individuals determine their particular fundamental goals. Fell's interpretation seems to me to be inconsistent with the doctrine that existence precedes essence, and fails to do justice to the numerous fundamental projects Sartre has mentioned. Cf. *BN*, pp. 566–67, where Sartre explicitly rejects the "single goal" interpretation of the desire to be God.

9. Also see Sartre, *Saint Genet*, p. 53.

difficulty would be even more acute if an attempt were made to specify which particular ends should be common to all men. Sartre would probably contend that a listing of such ends would presuppose the acceptance of some value framework or other. But the question is whether there can be any justification for accepting the entire framework. Sartre's account of the role of the individual project in our reason giving would imply that no such justification could be offered.

Freedom and the Fundamental Project

Sartre's concept of the fundamental project is as central to his theory of freedom as it is to his theory of rationality.[10] His theory of freedom has been misunderstood, however; so it makes sense to discuss a few of these misunderstandings before showing how the fundamental project functions within Sartre's view of freedom.

Mary Warnock, among others, has attacked Sartre's "extreme belief in freedom." Describing what she takes to be Sartre's position, she says there is an enormous range of freedom for human beings, who can not only do and feel as they choose but can "be whatever they choose."[11]

There are several difficulties with Mrs. Warnock's characterization of Sartre's position. In the first place, if she is discussing the concept of freedom developed in *Being and Nothingness*, which seems to be what she intended, then freedom to do what we choose is irrelevant. This, anyway, seems to be the point of Sartre's claim that "the slave in chains is as free as his master" (*BN*, 550). (This will be spelled out shortly.) On the other hand, if Mrs. Warnock is discussing later versions of Sartre's theory of freedom, the freedom-to-do is relevant, but the range of freedom is highly restricted.[12]

Since what she has in mind, however, seems to be the early

10. Sartre's theory of freedom has undergone some "radical conversions." Only the early view of freedom, developed in *Being and Nothingness*, is discussed here.
11. Mary Warnock, *The Philosophy of Sartre* (New York: Barnes & Noble, 1965), p. 10.
12. E.g., "Materialism and Revolution," pp. 237–38, where Sartre merely presents his earlier theory of freedom as a necessary condition of freedom.

"extreme" theory of freedom, it should be pointed out that Sartre discusses at some length the "resistance and obstacles" which human beings encounter but cannot overcome except by deciding on different purposes in relation to those brute givens. Thus, for example, "the rock appears to me in the light of a projected scaling . . . what my freedom cannot determine is whether the rock 'to be scaled' will or will not lend itself to scaling" (BN, 488). "There is freedom only in a *situation*," Sartre insists, and this situation, while it is organized and interpreted by us, includes a number of objective physical givens which would prevent our being free to do as we choose; place, body, past, and position are among these (BN, 489). None of these, however, poses a limit to human freedom, according to Sartre's early theory; the point is that freedom-to-do is not what Sartre meant at that time by freedom. He did not claim that human beings are omnipotent, as Mrs. Warnock appears to maintain.

On the other hand, Sartre did not mean freedom-to-do in the irrational manner required by an indeterminist position. As we noted earlier, he explicitly rejected an indeterminist position, in part because it renders the particular action "absurd" (BN, 437). He spells out the point that when he speaks of freedom he does not mean a "capricious, unlawful, gratuitous, and incomprehensible contingency" (BN, 453). In opposition to the indeterminist position, Sartre claims that "to speak of an act without a cause is to speak of an act which would lack the intentional structure of every act" (BN, 436–37). For Sartre, our chosen ends operate as a kind of final cause. The indeterminist position would not be relevant to moral decision making since it would view actions as occurring by chance. What is needed, however, is an agent who is responsible for—that is, causes—his own acts.

Sartre's body-subject is neither capricious nor passive with respect to external circumstances; rather, the individual is active. His reasons for acting are chosen from within what is given as brute fact; but the selected properties "have meaning only inside a projected ensemble which is precisely an ensemble of non-existents," that is, an organization of ends (BN, 437). The indeterminist position would make particular acts not only unpredictable but also unintelligible, since they could not be viewed as directed toward an end. Sartre maintains that it is false to make this claim about most human actions. His theory of freedom does not concern a freedom-to-do as we choose

either in a contracausal sense or in the sense that human beings
are omnipotent.

Warnock's statement that Sartre's view of freedom includes
the idea that people are free "to *be* whatever they choose" is
much closer to Sartre's actual theory of freedom, although it is
stated in a somewhat misleading fashion. Sartre's theory of
freedom is connected with the choice of an ideal self, but he
makes it clear that "success is not important to freedom" (*BN*,
483). That is, one is no less free in one's choice of self if one has
not fully realized the ideal self. When he says "man is a useless
passion," Sartre is insisting that the ideal self is in fact unreal-
izable (*BN*, 615). Warnock makes it sound, however, as if Sartre
thinks men are free in the sense of being able to fully realize—to
be—what they choose to be.

The other point that needs to be made explicit in reply to
Warnock is that a number of aspects of the person are objectively given and are not, as such, subject to our choice, for
instance, race, sex, class, nationality, physiological structure. It
is not a matter of choice that I am crippled, but it is a matter of
choice whether I make my disability an excuse for failure, or
something to be proud of, or a humiliation (*BN*, 328). Sartre
thinks we are free to choose ourselves in the sense of choosing
the self we want to be. But in other senses we are not in the
least free to choose what we are. One must distinguish between
those senses. In fairness to Sartre's critics, it should be added
that he does not always make these distinctions explicit and
that he sometimes misleadingly speaks as if freedom were "total."

A brief account of the central role of the fundamental
project within Sartre's theory of freedom can be given, insofar
as it is important to his concept of a person. We have seen that
Sartre's early theory of freedom is not based on freedom to do
as we choose, in either of the two senses discussed. What, then,
is the freedom Sartre discusses in *Being and Nothingness*? He
says "the fundamental act of freedom is . . . a choice of myself
in the world and by the same token it is a discovery of the
world" (*BN*, 461). This "choice of myself" has been discussed
as the choice of a fundamental project or ideal self.

This ideal self is the ultimate end or fundamental point of all
our actions, unless we choose another project; it is the relation
of co-personality that unites our actions and our experiences
into coherent patterns. The fundamental project is the ultimate
end in terms of which we give reasons and make decisions; it is,

in other words, the key to whatever rationality we exhibit. The choice of ideal self is also a "discovery of the world" in the sense that it serves as the point of our classification of things in the world as instruments, and the point of our classification of past events as meaningful.

It was suggested early in this study that Sartre might be interpreted as making the strong claim that all instances of conscious reference entail at least an implicit, if not explicit, reference to some state of affairs or end which does not exist. It should be apparent from this discussion of the fundamental project why he might make such a claim.

Sartre and Aristotle Compared

Other features of Sartre's concept of the fundamental project are still obscure, however. Some of these can be clarified by comparing Sartre's concept of the fundamental project with Aristotle's suggestion that there should be an over-all plan in life and by comparing their concepts of choice. While both Aristotle and Sartre offer a basically teleological approach, Aristotle appears to combine normative and descriptive considerations, but Sartre may be thinking of primarily descriptive ones. (I want to qualify this point later.) What I mean by this is that Aristotle thinks the ultimate end of action can be ascertained by describing the peculiar function of man, which is rational activity.[13] Later he says that if men are practically wise, they ought to plan and organize their lives in such a way as to attain that end.[14] When Sartre speaks of the individual's choice of a fundamental project, however, it is sometimes clear that he is not prescribing such a choice but is claiming that persons are in fact constituted by such choices of ultimate ends. I take this, at any rate, to be the point of his discussion of the need for an "existential psychoanalysis" which would *reveal* such choices of fundamental projects (*BN*, 571). Support for this point can also be found in recalling that Sartre tried to account for the *de facto* coherence of human personality, and for the factually

13. *Nicomachean Ethics*, I.7.1097^{b}20–25; I.7.1098^{a}5–8.
14. *Nicomachean Ethics*, VI.9.1142^{b}28–35; VI.8.1142^{a}8–12; VI.8. 1141^{b}28–35.

discoverable nonobjective features of remembering, by reference to the existence of a fundamental choice of project.

Certain difficulties arise, however, if we are correct in thinking that Sartre's theory of fundamental projects is intended to be primarily descriptive. One difficulty is that many people are not explicitly aware of having made such a choice of project, and Sartre himself has attacked the view that there are unconscious mental activities. If these points are taken into consideration, what does Sartre mean by saying we have *chosen* our fundamental project? If we have chosen a particular ideal self, why would an existential psychoanalysis be needed, in some cases, to bring this choice to light? What, for Sartre, *is* a choice?

Frederick Olafson has mentioned several points of contrast between the classic Aristotelian account of choice and the Sartrean account that can be cited in partial answer to this question. Olafson speaks first of the Aristotelian assumption that "choice must be a psychological event."[15] If we think that the question we are asking about choice is When did this inner event take place? then Sartre's account of choice will seem very unsatisfactory. But, says Olafson, the first point that needs to be understood about the existentialist concept of choice is that it is not an extra inner act but rather "a certain kind of *doing.*"[16]

Olafson's remark should be qualified by recalling that success is not a necessary feature of freedom. Sartre says "choice, being identical with acting, supposes a commencement of realization in order that the choice may be distinguished from the dream and the wish" (*BN*, 483). Presumably, then, an attempt to do y, as well as doing y, would count as a choice of y for Sartre. But we do not ordinarily make a mental choice in favor of project Y and *then* make the specific action-choices y_1, y_2, y_3, ... y_n. Frequently there are only the particular attempted and completed actions and thoughts which construct the project, not an additional superchoice. This means that unless we are reflectively aware of the *pattern* formed by our particular actions, it would be entirely possible not to know that we had chosen a fundamental project. Sartre insists that this would not mean that we were unconscious of this choice (*BN*, 570). But our awareness of it in such a case is prereflective; we are conscious

15. Frederick A. Olafson, *Principles and Persons: An Ethical Interpretation of Existentialism* (Baltimore: The Johns Hopkins Press, 1967), p. 163.
16. Ibid., p. 167.

of the fundamental project in the sense that we live it in our everyday actions and utterances (*BN*, 471). Others, who see our actions from the outside, may be able to see the total pattern more clearly than we can; and an existential psychoanalysis would enable us to take a semi-outside stance on our past acts to see where they were leading.

Another way of accounting for the fact that, in Sartre's view, we may not be explicitly aware of having made a choice of fundamental project can be obtained if we look at a further contrast mentioned by Olafson. He says the Aristotelian assumes that a choice can be made only after analysis of a situation has made explicit what alternatives are available. He points out that, for the existentialist, a choice is involved even in the original characterization of the situation.[17] The latter point can be spelled out as follows.

We may not be explicitly aware of the fundamental project we have chosen, since that choice focuses our original seeing of a situation as an instrumental complex. In our ordinary unreflective activities, we merely see the rock as "to be scaled," the nail as "to be driven into the wood." Sartre argued that it requires reflective awareness to see ourselves as having a given purpose with respect to the rock or nail. For Sartre it isn't necessarily the case that we make a fundamental choice of project as one of several alternatives within a situation; to the extent that we view the situation as embodying alternatives, these would ordinarily be different means of carrying out the project already chosen. The situation itself is a structured selection of certain characteristics of the objective environment. The choice of fundamental project is embodied in that selection and structuring.

Another important distinction between the Aristotelian and Sartrean concepts of choice also is mentioned by Olafson, who points out that the Aristotelian assumes that identification of action-relevant features of a situation can be controlled by "independently valid moral principles."[18] On the other hand, the existentialist holds that we cannot derive our evaluations from any more fundamental truths, and that we must therefore recognize that what we count as reasons have been chosen as such by us.

The discussion can be carried one step beyond Olafson's account. Another way of emphasizing the difference between

17. Ibid., pp. 163, 164.
18. Ibid., pp. 163–65.

Aristotle and Sartre is to mention that one point of apparent agreement between them conceals a profound disagreement. Both Aristotle and Sartre claim that—in Aristotle's words—"we deliberate not about ends but about means."[19] In the case of the final end, which now is our special concern, Sartre and Aristotle differ sharply about why we do not deliberate about it. For Aristotle, the point is that the final end is given; there is no room for deliberations, since we "ascertain" the rational function of man. We can deliberate only where we can choose, Aristotle says, and we can choose means, not ends.[20]

For Sartre, however, the reason why we cannot deliberate about fundamental ends is that the very reasons we would use in deliberation presuppose a choice of the fundamental project within which some consideration might count as a reason. The initial choice is "unjustifiable" in the sense that no reasons can be given for it; once a particular project has been chosen, we can deliberate about what would be conducive to that end. But the final end cannot be ascertained cognitively since there is no such given final end (*BN*, 461–65).[21]

It should be noted that Sartre, in effect, argues that there are two different levels of choice making. At the level of the fundamental project, a choice is made without deliberation since there are no interproject reasons which would enable one to decide between fundamental projects. But once a project has been chosen, particular choices can be justified by reference to the fundamental project. Voluntary deliberation can certainly take place within this framework, since on this level a decision has been made about what will count as a reason (*BN*, 445).

It is tempting to try to refute Sartre by pointing out that there is a period in adolescence when most people appear to be deliberating when they try to list the reasons for being, say, a lawyer against the reasons for being a plumber. This need not count against Sartre's description of the choice of fundamental project.

In the first place, if these deliberations led to a choice, Sartre might argue that they could do so because the chosen career is not usually identical with the individual's fundamental project. To be sure, Sartre sometimes mentions a project which seems to

19. *Nicomachean Ethics*, III.3.1.1112^{b}13; cf, *BN*, p. 444.
20. *Nicomachean Ethics*, I.7.1097^{b}23–1098^{a}18; III.3.1113^{a}3–5.
21. Cf. R. M. Hare, *The Language of Morals* (New York: Oxford University Press, 1964), p. 69. Hare points out that justification comes to an end when the inquirer is faced with a decision whether or not to accept a way of life. Once accepted, justification can be based on that way of life.

be a career, as when he describes his own fundamental project as that of being a writer. But Sartre does not seem to be speaking here of a career in the narrow sense in which we work to make a living; he seems to have broadened the use of the "career term" to mean a more general and basic world outlook which operates to bring one's life closer to the universally desired godlike unity and permanence. In such a case one would expect (and would find, in Sartre's case) that not only his work but his recreation, friendships, political commitments, etc., would be informed by that fundamental choice of being a writer. Whatever operates as the ultimate point of an individual's deliberations, shaping his particular choices into a coherent pattern, deserves the title "fundamental project." In some cases, although surely not typically, this might be the individual's life work.

In the aforementioned case of the adolescent, it may be that his fundamental project was to become rich, which would have given a point to his deliberations without being an outcome of those deliberations. Thus his career choice could be made after deliberation because there was another underlying goal in terms of which one career seemed more promising than the other.

On the other hand, there might not have been any way for the adolescent to decide between various alternatives. He might have found himself struggling with conflicting sets of considerations, unable to decide. It is open to Sartre to say that the individual has not yet made his choice of a fundamental project in such a case. It was pointed out earlier that Sartre appears to discuss the fundamental project as if it were discoverable and describable, and this should now be qualified by saying that the description seems to apply to human beings only after a certain point in their lives. The infant is not born with a fundamental project. For instance, Jean Genet is described by Sartre as having been ten years old when he assumed as his fundamental project the label "thief,"[22] but it might have been at an earlier or later age. We certainly recognize that there is a period in childhood before a child's actions have achieved any large degree of integration. We speak of the child's character as not yet formed, whereas Sartre would say that the fundamental project has not yet been chosen.

Sartre appears to be able to handle the case of the adolescent who is deliberating. On the other hand, certain other objections could be made against the descriptive claim that there is a

22. Sartre, *Saint Genet*, p. 26.

choice of a fundamental project in the life of individuals. In the first place, many people live their entire lives in the state of mind of the confused adolescent, unable to decide what they most want to do. Other people may have decided what they want to be but appear to be unable to achieve the degree of organization required to carry out the decision. Other people appear to be fairly stable, but also have to be described as having chosen several fundamental projects. While the greatest value of Sartre's discussion of the choice of fundamental project seems to be that it offers a plausible way of accounting for a number of facts, there seems to be a limit to the applicability of this account.

He has discussed the choice of fundamental project as a way of accounting for the fact that human beings exhibit a variety of purposes and a corresponding variety of reasons; for the fact that people's actions are, on the whole, intelligible, if not predictable in detail; for the fact that sometimes abrupt character changes occur; and for the fact that perceiving and remembering are selective and purposive. The first two examples (above) suggest, however, that Sartre's account is not universally applicable. The perpetually confused and the chronically inadequate do not appear to be describable as individuals who have made a choice of fundamental project. This may not be a serious objection, however; surely color-blind individuals do not invalidate an account of color vision in individuals who can see the normal range of colors.

There is some reason to think Sartre intends to offer a prescription in the cases which are not describable within his view. I have avoided emphasizing this point until now, since popular discussions of existentialism tend to ignore its descriptive claims and to emphasize the notion of "commitment" as if it were a solely prescriptive concept. Some of Sartre's popular works support this interpretation, as they include such phrases as "first I ought to commit myself and then act my commitment."[23] Another interpretation of this phrase, however, might be that we ought to become explicitly aware of the fundamental choice of project we have in fact made, in order to be more effective in carrying it out. The phrase is an odd one, not only because it appears to treat the notion of commitment prescriptively but also because Sartre speaks as if commitment were an inner event prior to action, which elsewhere he seems to deny. It is difficult to know how much weight to place on

23. Sartre, "Existentialism Is a Humanism," p. 299.

any phrase in this essay in view of the fact that Sartre regretted its publication as "*une 'erreur.'* "[24]

A final comparison can be made between Sartre's view of the fundamental project and Aristotle's suggestion that we should plan and organize our lives around a final end. In discussing this comparison I will assume that Sartre may have meant not only that most people make choices of a fundamental project but also that they ought to make such choices if they have not done so. The comparison in this case concerns the content, rather than the nature, of choice.

W. F. R. Hardie has pointed out a confusion in Aristotle's conception of a single final end. Hardie suggests the need for distinguishing two kinds of final end: an inclusive end and a dominant end. He points out that Aristotle explicitly defends the notion that the final end is dominant, that is, the object of one prime desire. Hardie also points out that it is rare, in fact, to discover a man who has organized his life in such a way as to satisfy "one ruling passion."[25] If we treat Aristotle's final end as a dominant end, and attempt to prescribe the good life on the basis of attaining it, the obvious difficulty is that the best life for man could not possibly be the achievement of one goal to the exclusion of all others. At times, however, Aristotle seems to mean that the final end is an inclusive end, that is, a "comprehensive plan" which would be a "full and harmonious achievement of primary ends."[26] Hardie suggests that Aristotle might have seen deliberation as having a role in the choice of ends, if the latter doctrine had been consistently carried through.[27]

The same question can be asked about Sartre's fundamental project. Does he claim that we do (or should) make a choice of fundamental project which is a dominant end, that is, which excludes all other ends? When Sartre gives examples of fundamental projects, it would be easy to interpret him in this way at many points. He has mentioned, for instance, choices of being a thief or of being inferior to others. Frequently, also, Sartre uses the singular form to refer to the final end, as in the phrase "my ultimate and initial project" (*BN*, 463). If this choice were a

24. Francis Jeanson, *Le Problème Moral et la Pensée de Sartre*, lettre-préface de Jean-Paul Sartre (Paris: Editions du Seuil, 1965), p. 36.

25. W. F. R. Hardie, "The Final Good in Aristotle's *Ethics*," in *Aristotle: A Collection of Critical Essays*, ed. J. M. E. Moravcsik (Garden City, N.Y.: Doubleday, 1967), pp. 298–300.

26. Ibid., p. 300.

27. Ibid., p. 302.

choice of a dominant end that excludes all others, Hardie's criticisms of Aristotle would be applicable to Sartre's view. It could be pointed out that in fact very few people are ruled by a consuming passion for one and only one end, and we could use the example of stable people who have successfully integrated more than one major career as a counterexample to Sartre's descriptive claim that there is a choice of a single fundamental project. And Hardie's criticism, that the good life surely cannot consist in fulfilling one end to the exclusion of all other ends, would be very much to the point. Sartre's descriptive claim would be unbelievable, and his prescription would be unacceptable, if the choice of fundamental project were a choice of a dominant end.

There is good textual evidence, however, in support of the claim that Sartre did not mean the fundamental project is a narrow and exclusive end. He speaks, for instance, of "my ultimate and total possibility, as the original integration of all my particular possibles" (*BN*, 461). Again, he speaks of "a projected ensemble which is precisely an ensemble of non-existents," that is, a grouping of ends (*BN*, 437). He has spoken of the self as "an harmonious integration of enterprises in the external world."[28] He explicitly criticizes the social expectation that a man confine himself within the demands of his job situation (*BN*, 59). Sartre's biting attack on the narrowness and rigidity of social attempts to reduce one's interests strongly suggests that he does not think of the fundamental project as a dominant end which operates to exclude other purposes. Sartre's own fundamental project, that of being a writer, has certainly not meant that he writes all day long, seven days a week, to the exclusion of every other activity. It is as a writer, rather than as an elected official, that he makes a contribution to the political life of his country; it was as a writer, not as a soldier, that he fought the Nazis when he was in prison camp; it is as a writer that he has traveled, made friends, gone to peace conferences.[29] The fundamental project appears to function as a top-priority end which sets the stage for working out other purposes. All of the other ends are connected and unified through this project.

Sartre's concept of the choice of a fundamental project appears to be an alternative to two other possibilities. It is an

28. Sartre, *Psychology of Imagination*, p. 223.
29. Simone de Beauvoir, *Force of Circumstance*, trans. Richard Howard (New York: G. P. Putnam, 1964), p. 41.

alternative to the reduction of life to a single dominant end, such as the career role society expects of us. It is an alternative, also, to the fragmentation that would result if we developed wholly separate systems of relations for our work, our play, our friendships, etc. If the fundamental project could be fully realized, the result would be that I "at last become a whole man."[30]

But Sartre has said that the fundamental project cannot be fully realized, which brings us full circle to our starting point. The project is the relation of co-personality which unites successive actions into a system of relations. It is a substitute for the permanence and wholeness which would characterize the god-like immaterial person-substance, if there were such an entity. The self we construct, however, is always incomplete and could be abandoned at any time.

Some Objections

Several objections have been and can be raised in connection with Sartre's account of character, fundamental choice of project, and the role of the fundamental project in the formation of character. Alvin Plantinga has offered the criticism that it is logically impossible for Sartre to make a wrong choice, since Sartre claims that both value and rationality are defined by choice. Since Plantinga thinks that any act which conflicted with the original choice of fundamental project would simply represent a new aboriginal choice, all actions and choices are right by definition. Morality thus becomes impossible.[31]

Sartre's implicit distinction between two levels of choice making would permit him to give a partial reply to Plantinga's criticism. At the level of the choice of fundamental project,

---

30. Jean-Paul Sartre, *The Words*, trans. Bernard Frechtman (Greenwich, Conn.: Fawcett Publications, 1964), p. 121. Cf. supra: "man is a totality and not a collection." Sartre's terminology is confusing, to say the least. When Sartre claims that man is a totality, he is saying of the person, *qua* system of relations, that it is organized. When he denies that man could be whole, however, he is denying that that organization of conscious relations is ever complete while the man lives. Sartre frequently uses the qualifying expression "detotalized totality" to indicate the permanent incompleteness of the person *qua* system of relations (*BN*, pp. 622–24).

31. See Alvin Plantinga, "An Existentialist's Ethics," *Review of Metaphysics*, 12, no. 2 (December 1958): 245–49.

Plantinga is certainly correct in claiming that value and rationality are defined. Sartre would also agree that universal morality is thus rendered highly improbable, if not impossible. Sartre's point, however, is that there *are* many moralities. Furthermore, he might point out that even similar moral beliefs may occupy a much different status in the hierarchy of values of the individual whose fundamental goal is to be a Christian than their status within the system of someone whose Christianity is peripheral to his fundamental goal of being a business entrepreneur. Descriptively speaking, Sartre seems correct in claiming there are many moral systems—however uncomfortable this fact may be for the moral philosopher.

But Plantinga errs, I believe, in thinking that a new aboriginal choice of project is necessarily given in the single act which conflicts with the original project, for that choice is given in the series and not in the single act. The point was made earlier that there can be uncharacteristic acts even though most of one's actions tend in a certain direction. This is an important point for Sartre because he uses it to counter the claim, made by many philosophers, that character produces actions. Within the framework of a given fundamental project, Sartre can certainly claim that certain acts are evil or stupid.

If my fundamental project is to be a writer, it is just plain dumb for me to pawn my typewriter to buy tickets for the World Series. This need not mean, however, that my fundamental project is abandoned, although (depending on the subsequent pattern of my actions) it might signal the beginning of a new project or a modification of the old one. We can know that my project continues if we observe my repeated labors to produce longhand manuscripts, my eventual steps to sell the family jewels so I can get the typewriter back, etc. Only if my subsequent acts show me to be an avid sports fan (in contrast to my earlier indifference) would we speak of a new aboriginal choice or a new choice which modified the original choice. In the one case I give up writing in favor of sports; in the other case I continue to write, but I write about sports instead of politics. Again, my original choice to become a Christian is not abandoned if I keep trying to be kind after a regretted fit of temper.

Since a fundamental project continues to be the final end as long as a certain trend of ideas and actions continues, there can certainly be occasional uncharacteristic acts which might be judged wrong within that framework. The fundamental goal would provide direction for most of the acts one did, and in this sense, also, it would operate as a standard or as a moral ideal. Unless Plantinga's point is that only universalizable values can be considered moral, it does not seem to me that Sartre makes morality impossible.

Another criticism is connected with the fact that the single act, such as the aforementioned boy's resistance to threats, may be placed under a variety of descriptions. Isn't there, then, a problem in deciding what someone's fundamental project is? Sartre does not wish to speak of fundamental goals' being discoverable on the basis of the single act, but the same ambiguity which is present in the single act can be present in each act of the person. Thus, couldn't the critic wonder whether there was ever a single series which could be said to lend coherence to the person's character?

Part of a reply could be based on that element of the ambiguity in the boy's act, which was due to being taken out of the context of his other actions. But some ambiguity still remains, and this is just what we all face in our attempts to assess ourselves and other people.

There is, I believe, such a problem, but Sartre could claim that it does not in any way originate with his account of character and choice of project. For instance, his friends describe Harry as a bold revolutionary who acts with vigor on behalf of student freedom. The administrators of Harry's school are divided, however, for some see him as a clever political subversive while others view his actions as those of an insubordinate and spoiled child. It may be that Harry himself has a totally different interpretation of his actions. For reasons which will become clearer in the next chapter, Sartre is unwilling to say Harry's view of his action series is the correct one. In fact, Sartre has no clear way of deciding which, if any, of these alternatives points toward the real fundamental project.

A similar problem is faced by the existential psychotherapist who wishes to understand the tightly organized world of his psychotic patient, except that the problem may be for the therapist to get outside his own customary view of reality in order to attempt to discover the fundamental project which has given structure to his patient's world. Usually, however, we interpret others partly in terms of our own fundamental projects, selecting those aspects of their actions and utterances which make sense to us in the light of our own goals; part of that interpretation is based on what they actually do, which we can see as tending toward goals of their own. These difficulties of interpretation do not prevent our seeing patterns in the actions of others; in fact, we would be very likely to revise our estimate of them if we did not find additional acts which support our original judgment and if all their ensuing acts seem to be incompatible with what we first thought about them. Harry's friends, but also the unsympathetic administrators, see a coherent pattern in Harry's fiery speeches to his fellow undergraduates, his petitions, etc. But they place very different values on those acts and on his goal, as they perceive them.

These examples suggest that the ambiguity inherent in descriptions of the single act does not preclude the strong likelihood that considerable coherence in the behavior of ourselves and others can be found. But they also suggest—what may in fact be true—that there is no single correct description of a person's fundamental project. This may be an uncomfortable conclusion for the philosopher who espouses universal values, but it is not therefore an obviously false conclusion. It may also be an uncomfortable conclusion for the therapist whose theory requires an objective distinction between what is real and what his psychotic patient perceives as real. Sartre does not offer clear criteria for making such a distinction.

Maybe the therapist does not need such a distinction, however, if he can admit that the "normal" view of reality varies from culture to culture, from time to time, and from profession to profession. It is very different for the twentieth-century American from what it was for the fifth-century B.C. Greek, and very different for B. F. Skinner from what it is for the contemporary civil libertarian.

Still another objection can be raised in connection with psychological problems, and this leads to a serious problem for Sartre's view. Psychologists sometimes distinguish between acts which are unfree, in the sense that they are compulsive, and those which are done without compulsion. If we suppose that compulsive acts can be performed repeatedly, and thus can form regular patterns, it appears that Sartre's account asks us to conclude from the young woman's repeated acts of handwashing that she had chosen a fundamental project which includes cleanliness as at least one element.

Sartre's account of character can handle part of the criticism but perhaps not the most important part. If the criticism suggests that the young woman's feeling of being compelled is sufficient evidence for her lack of freedom, it can be recalled that Sartre's distinction between two levels of choice making gave us a way of suggesting that introspective evidence can be misleading. One's basic freedom is in the choice of fundamental project, but, given that long-range choice, certain steps may be given as leading, more or less effectively, to a fulfillment of that goal. There may be little or no choice in those steps in some cases. Or again, Sartre says we may be blind to the actual tendency of a series of acts if we have failed to reflect on it. Any of these points within Sartre's position may help to account for the sense of compulsion the young lady has. In such a case, therapy might be directed toward getting her to see and to admit her fundamental choice in order to discover whether she wishes to continue that project or to restructure the meaning of her past and present life events in the light of a new choice.

Furthermore, Sartre is not committed to saying that an action series must be described literally; he insists, in fact, that acts have symbolic meaning (*BN*, 568). Thus if the critic thinks he has trapped Sartre because the handwashing has only a symbolic meaning (e.g. she really seeks freedom from guilt and not physical cleanliness), the critic has failed to see that any given action series must be interpreted within the context of the patient's total project.

In another type of case, however, it seems to me that Sartre has not given us a way of answering the critic. If Sartre is correct in claiming that the body-subject acts and chooses, there is the strong possibility that at least some action series are not the outcome of normally functioning synthetic brain activity. The critic is not even required to claim that all acts are determined by prior and external events, for he might admit that the brain's selectivity ordinarily enables the individual to act according to his choices.

The problem for Sartre is that some repeated actions result from physiological abnormalities. His claim that we are totally free in the choice of fundamental project, and thus totally responsible, breaks down in the face of evidence that some habitually violent people may suffer from chromosome abnormalities which apparently leave no room for active choice of an end. Even if the individual in question felt free in committing that violence, it would not help Sartre, since he has pointed out that introspective evidence of this sort can be deceptive.

It does not seem to me that such physiological evidence can immediately be extended to support the claim that no human behavior is responsible, or even that no one is responsible for criminal behavior. But Sartre fails to give us *any* criteria for distinguishing the physiologically controlled series of acts from the series which is performed in the attempt to bring about a chosen end. The distinction is crucial for purposes of assigning moral and legal responsibility, and thus the gap is serious.

Still another problem would arise if a critic were to ask whether it is plausible to claim, as Sartre sometimes claims, that all acts and utterances are directed toward a single fundamental project. This claim, in its strong and apparently universal form ("man . . . expresses himself as a whole in even his most insignificant and his most superficial behavior" [*DN*, 568]), is made in the context of a comparison between the Freudian and existential forms of psychoanalysis. They are similar approaches to the extent that they seek symbolic meaning in each and every act and utterance. Taken as a universal claim, however, this seems to contradict Sartre's point that there can be uncharacteristic actions—a point which is important in the attempt to show that character does not produce actions.

Maybe this can be explained away by the rather plausible suggestion that an uncharacteristic act is known to be such only in relation to the fundamental project, and the doer of such an act makes this clear in his expressions of regret, annoyance, etc. This seems to me only somewhat plausible, however, and the strong form of the claim seems to be less defensible than the modified version of the claim, which we have also discussed. Sartre sometimes speaks as if character possesses only a relatively high degree of coherence, and as if most (not all) acts are to be taken as forming the characteristic patterns which constitute a choice of project.

If we take this as a description rather than as a prescription, it seems to me that there are serious problems with the claim even in its weaker form. For one thing, there seem to be a large number of daily activities which most of us perform and which do not appear to have any special bearing on the individual's fundamental project: buying and reading the paper, walking the dog, washing the car, brushing one's teeth, etc. If one were simply to count the number of acts performed and/or the hours spent in such activities, it may well be that these activities take up the bulk of one's waking and nonworking hours. Furthermore, if one's fundamental project is totally different from the job one has taken in order to survive, one's fundamental project may be given little or no time in an average day. The working day is spent, say, in the factory and in getting to and from work, but perhaps the fundamental goal for which one lives is to read all the novels ever written.

The frequency of those acts tending in a certain direction

does not seem to be an adequate criterion for the correct designation of fundamental choices, given that most people may need to order their lives in ways that have little or nothing to do with what they want to be but a great deal to do with the bare necessity of staying alive and keeping their families alive.

The quantitative principle as such does not permit Sartre to handle certain other types of problems in the application of character predicates.[32] Suppose that one wishes to speak of Jones as a kind man, and that kindness is one of the essential traits within the compass of his fundamental project: to be a good Christian. Sartre's Summary Theory would suggest that to speak of him as kind is to say that at t_1 he did a favor for Mrs. S, and that at t_2 he helped an old man across the street, and that at t_3 he released an indigent family man from a debt, etc. Let us also suppose that he had had a few temper outbursts which were out of proportion to the situations but that, by and large, people count on Jones for favors and charitable contributions, and he usually meets those expectations. The theory seems to work well in this case.

But suppose that ninety-nine times out of a hundred Jones acts kindly, but that once a year, or even once every five years, he kills someone. Let us suppose that the circumstances of the killings preclude the possibility of their being mercy killings, and let us try to treat them simply as out-of-character acts. Brandt's earlier example may be turned around to suggest that while no single act is sufficient ground for a justified judgment about character, a single act *of a certain type* might be enough to call into question a quantitatively justified judgment about a man's character.

Taking another type of trait, can we make a purely quantitative judgment with respect to a man's being a homosexual if 75 percent of his experiences are homosexual and 25 percent are heterosexual? In this case, "bisexual" seems to be the more appropriate designation; but at what point—what percentage—does one or the other sex-preference characterization become accurate? Is a man honest if 75 percent of his acts are honest but 25 percent are dishonest? Probably not; we would usually call him dishonest. Curiously, however, we would definitely call him dishonest if the percentages were reversed.

These examples suggest some reasons for doubting that Sartre's Summary Theory can be accepted in a purely quantita-

32. This line of criticism was suggested to me by an unpublished paper, "Character and Action," by Norvin Richards.

tive form. It should be noted and emphasized that none of these examples offers even remote support for his opponent's claim that character produces actions. However, they all suggest the need for clear limits to the applicability of the claim that we can describe a man's character patterns and ascertain his fundamental choice of project by discovering the relative frequency of those acts which tend toward a given goal. They also suggest the need for distinguishing different types of acts with respect to spelling out the relevant qualitative as well as additional quantitative aspects (e.g., a sharp retort weighs much less heavily against an attribution of kindness than does a sadistic murder).

The above suggestions are not incompatible with a modified form of the Summary Theory of character, but they suggest that Sartre's theory is in need of clarification if it is to work. It seems to me that the fundamental project may provide Sartre a rough way of introducing qualitative considerations. Thus one must consider not only the frequency but the relevance and importance of a series of acts in relation to a particular fundamental project, as well as the relevance and importance of acts which go counter to this project. Any summary of past acts, then, would include qualitative as well as quantitative elements.

If the considerations offered in this critical discussion are good, then the coherence of the self we construct is, descriptively speaking, usually only a relative coherence at best. Taken as a prescription, it may fare a little better if we assume that he means we should, ideally, seek greater integration of our enterprises and activities.

At this point, discussion of Sartre's concept of a person is nearly complete, but one question in particular has remained unanswered. It was shown earlier that the capacity for reflection is central to Sartre's discussion of some uses of "I," but no explanation has yet been offered how it is that people can take a reflective look at themselves. This point will be discussed in the course of considering what Sartre says about our ways of knowing other minds exist.

Chapter 6

The Existence of Other Minds

Before concluding this discussion of Sartre's concept of a person we will take a brief look at what he has to say about our awareness of the existence of others. One purpose of this chapter will be to lay bare the basic premises with which Sartre is working and to formulate his arguments. Since most of these premises have been discussed earlier in connection with his criteria of identity for persons, it will be necessary only to indicate how Sartre also uses them in this discussion. Another purpose of this chapter will be to show how Sartre accounts for the important capacity to reflect. It was suggested earlier that this ability in human beings is a condition of their being able to evaluate their actions and to formulate alternative purposes.

From Sartre's viewpoint, two mistaken assumptions have led to an incorrect formulation of the question of the existence of other minds. One of these, which will be discussed later, is the unqualified supposition that we are certain of our own existence. The second assumption is that there is some kind of gap between the observable human body and the consciousness that may or may not be hidden inside that human form and that may or may not contain a thought or experience. Thus it is frequently assumed that knowledge of physical things is much firmer than our merely inferential knowledge of conscious things.

Sartre denies that there is a gap. He says "being-for-others is wholly body; there are no 'psychic phenomena' there to be united with the body. There is nothing *behind* the body. But the body is wholly 'psychic' " (*BN*, 305).

Part of what Sartre means in calling the human body "psychic" is just that it is the subject of conscious experiences. The other-minds problem is generated in part by the prevalent assumption that the other's mind is hidden inside the other's body and that it is like a "closed box" containing intentional objects, sensations, etc. (*BN*, 314). Sartre's arguments against this view have already been presented. An important corollary of the prevailing assumption that minds are private boxes, however, is that we sometimes think experiences are hidden contents, whose existence in others can only be inferred or believed on the basis of a weak analogy with our own case.

Sartre would say that the very formulation of the problem of the existence of others has been at fault. Much of the contemporary discussion has centered on how I can know that X has a particular experience, such as pain. Hector-Neri Castañeda gives a succinct formulation of some of the central assumptions of the debate when he says that our thinking that someone has a mind is to think that he is conscious, and to think that someone is conscious is to attribute an experience or thought to him. Castañeda adds that what knowledge we have of other minds is inferential.[1]

Sartre does not deny that we have organic sensations which are accessible only to the individual who feels them.[2] The body-subject can take its own states as objects of awareness. What he denies is that a given private sensation is all that is meant, or even the most important part of what is meant, when we say that someone is conscious. Sartre insists, rather, on "the organized character of emotion."[3] That is to say, when we speak of hatred or anger or even pain, we do not refer to a particular felt sensation. Rather, we are speaking of a system of responses, one of whose elements may (or may not) be a private sensation, but many of whose elements are visible behaviors, organized with certain ends in view and taking place within a certain observable situation.[4]

To support his claim that terms for private sensations are not an essential part of the meaning of emotion-words, Sartre points out that anger or hatred can exist as dispositions even in the absence of a particular sensation at any given time. Pain can also

1. Hector-Neri Castañeda, "Consciousness and Behavior: Their Basic Connections," in *Intentionality, Minds and Perception*, ed. Hector-Neri Castañeda (Detroit: Wayne State University Press, 1967), p. 123.

2. As noted earlier, however, Sartre would deny the commonly accepted view that privacy of sensation necessarily implies a mental phenomenon. For example, the body-subject can directly know the spatial position his right foot occupies in relation to his left foot, even if he cannot observe either foot.

3. Sartre, *The Emotions*, p. 42.

4. Cf. Don Locke's distinction between "being in pain" and "feeling a pain." Locke admits that behavioral criteria are sufficient grounds for saying someone *is* in pain, although not for someone's feeling a pain (*Myself and Others: A Study in Our Knowledge of Minds* [London: Clarendon Press of Oxford University Press, 1968], p. 66). Sartre would insist that if the question is whether another is conscious, then his being in pain is all that we need to know.

exist as a disposition, as in a long illness; that is, many of the activities during the period of the illness—taking medicine, avoiding drafts, etc.—can be understood in terms of the desire to avoid or to mitigate moments of recurring felt pain (*BN*, 336).

Furthermore, there has been common acceptance of the idea that someone can act in such a way as to exhibit "unconscious" love or hatred. As we saw, Sartre substitutes the prereflective/reflective and objective/interpretive distinctions for the mechanism of the unconscious mind as a means of explaining these actions, but he could point to them as further examples of the fact that we ascribe emotions on the basis of a behavior pattern even when there is definitely no accompanying private sensation.

According to Sartre, it is not necessary to find out whether someone is having a particular thought or a particular experience at a given time, although this may be an interesting question in its own right. However, if we want to know whether X is conscious, we need not ask whether X has a specific, unobservable thought or experience in his private mental box. Behavioral criteria are sufficient to establish that he is angry at George or that he loves this woman—not that a man feels anger or a twinge of love. If we wish to find out whether X is conscious, we need only ask whether he sustains observable intentional relations with objects and with other people. This is the approach that underlies Sartre's first argument.

When he speaks of the human body as "psychic," Sartre means the body is the conscious subject; in addition, he means that conscious behavior is observable as such. While we cannot see the physical relation "taller than," we can observe *that* the Empire State Building is taller than the building to the south of it. While we cannot observe the intentional relation "conscious of *a* for the purpose of *y*," we can surely see *that* Jones screams, stamps, and makes threatening gestures toward Smith. We can also observe that these acts take place within certain action sequences, and on a stage or following the crash of Smith's car into Jones' fender. For Sartre, anger behavior is the anger itself, not merely the sign of something else which is hidden from view.[5]

5. Cf. J. L. Austin, "Other Minds," in *Logic and Language: Second Series*, ed. Antony Flew (Garden City, N.Y.: Doubleday, 1965), p. 372. Austin points out that we don't in fact believe that we are aware only of signs or symptoms of another's anger; rather, we contrast "signs" with the actual behavioral display of anger.

In other words, the screams and fist waving do not refer to a private sensation; they refer to a context within which they make sense, and to additional items of behavior: more gestures, more cries, a punch in the nose.

Sartre admits that we can be mistaken and can take for genuine anger what is actually only an act or a pretense. But what are we mistaken about? Other observable acts, or perhaps the situation within which the acts occurred. We had understood his gesture as an intention to strike, but what Jones actually does is stop, laugh, and say that this is what the villain in the movies did (BN, 294, 346).

For Sartre, consciousness is a form of relation to the world, not a private container. To be angry is not just to feel an isolated internal content but to be related angrily—that is, with shouts, blows or coldness, rather than with caresses—to some object or person in order to achieve some end.[6] One must observe a series of actions to find out how a yell or a grimace fits into that series; one must observe the situation within which an action is performed to find out the point of that action. If a grimace is preceded by the person's stating "Now I'll show you how a man in pain looks," of course we would not expect an organic sensation to accompany the next moment's facial expression. Within this particular situation and action series, the grimace is a kind of joke performed by a conscious human being who intended to amuse us. Put slightly differently, Sartre claims that behavioral phenomena are at least part, and in some cases all, of what we mean when we say someone is angry or that someone loves someone else.

A frequent mistake has been to assume that one ought to be able to isolate particular physical manifestations and connect them (vertically, as it were) to particular private sensations. Sartre would deny that there is a logical connection in the sense usually discussed, that is, a one-to-one correspondence between each item of behavior and a specific private sensation. The alleged need to make an inference to something unknown depends in part on this mistaken assumption. But our knowledge of the other's conscious relations to the things and people around him is at least as firmly grounded as our knowledge of his physical characteristics.

The relation between conscious existents can take two basic

6. This is how Sartre distinguishes his position from that of the behaviorists of his time; the latter fail to take into account the intentionality of the other (BN, p. 294).

forms, depending on whether I intend the other as an object or whether he intends me as an object. These will be discussed separately. If I intend the other as an object, then "the appearance among the objects of *my* universe of an element of disintegration in that universe is what I mean by the appearance of a man in my universe" (*BN*, 255). This form of the relation does not yield certainty of the other's existence. The point has been made in recent literature on personal identity that we see others as acting purposefully, and that the ground for ascribing consciousness to others is observation of their behavior.[7] Sartre agrees that this is one basis for ascribing consciousness, but he goes beyond these points to give an account of what we mean when we say we see another acting purposefully. For this reason, Sartre's first argument is interesting even though it does not purport to give certainty of the other's existence.

His subsidiary argument can be paraphrased as follows:

1. My world is an instrumental complex; that is, objects appear to me as organized in relation to my body as center and in relation to my ends (*BN*, 325).

2. Individual physical objects appear to me as belonging to that totality of instruments which I have organized (*BN*, 200).

3. At times I discover that an object which belongs within my instrumental complex has acquired a use which places it within another system of uses (*BN*, 254).

4. The loss of the object disintegrates my instrumental complex; that is, an object which I needed, or which I saw as being related to purposes of my own, and being a certain distance from my body, must now be regarded as having another use and being a certain distance from another body (*BN*, 254–55).

5. Nonconscious existents cannot arrange physical objects for their use. (*BN*, 254).

Conclusion: Another conscious existent has invented an alien use for "my" object; I perceive the other as conscious through his reclassification of elements in my instrumental complex (*BN*, 253–57, 339).

Sartre points out that he is not referring to "any mystic or ineffable experience" (*BN*, 253). The common, everyday objects

7. E.g., Strawson, *Individuals*, pp. 102, 108.

of experience are what we see as instruments, and what we can lose as instruments. This may be clarified by an example.

When Sartre speaks of organizing objects into an instrumental complex he means this in the sense of "seeing-as," but probably also in the sense of physically arranging things to suit our purposes. Assuming this is so, if I am an artist I can arrange objects with the intention of painting them from a certain point where my body will be. Accordingly, I arrange the lighting, paints, easel, and objects on a table; these include a glass of water placed at the precise point where it will catch certain subtle reflections and will partially block a grouping of fruit at the angle from which I will see these objects when I stand at the easel. Suppose now that my friend Peter walks into the room, says "I'm thirsty," and takes my glass of water and drinks it. This disintegration of my arrangement of things brings me into direct confrontation and conflict with Peter as a conscious existent who has used an object in my instrumental complex as a means to the end of satisfying his thirst.

Sartre would certainly have to admit that something nonconscious, for example an earthquake, might have disturbed my arrangement of objects; but in this case there would be no reintegration of the object into another system of uses. The objects would have been shattered and useless. In the example, however, the glass of water is given another use, an alien use, in relation to another person. But the critic can easily point out that an animal, instead of a person, could have come on the scene and drunk the water, or a robot, programmed to construct an artificial lake, might have carried away my object in order to carry out the next step in his instructions. For these reasons, as well as for a reason acknowledged by Sartre, this particular line of argument is not conclusive.

Our experience of the loss of an object, with the ensuing disintegration of the world as we have organized it, might be considered partial evidence for the existence of others as conscious. Sartre does not consider this evidence certain, however, because in this case we are dealing with the other who is acting in the midst of physical objects. He has said that our knowledge of the existence of physical objects is never stronger than highly probable (*BN*, 254). It should be emphasized that while Sartre contends that we can observe others acting intentionally in relation to the objects and people around them, he says that consciousness as such is "inapprehensible" (*BN*, 408). Just because the other's consciousness is not directly available to our sense experience, Sartre says it is a mistake to treat the other *qua* conscious as an object whose existence is only probable. Alvin Plantinga, for instance, discussed whether the existence of others is "more probable than not on my total evidence."[8]

It is a misapplication of the concept of probability, however, to try to use it in such a case. Sartre points out that the concept of probability is applicable only when we are dealing with objects of sense experience, and when such experience could in principle yield new evidence leading to the validation or invalidation of one's hypothesis. For this reason, he insists that the other must be immediately given as conscious, and that his existence must be "as sure as my own" if there is to be any point to the claim that we know the other (*BN*, 235, 250–51). Insofar as the other is an observable being, of course, he can be treated as an object of knowledge whose existence is highly probable. But Sartre points out that the solipsist could admit that much. Thus far, then, the discussion of Sartre's position has shown only that our knowledge of the other as conscious is not weaker than our knowledge of physical beings.

Beyond this, Sartre seeks an account of our *certainty* of the existence of the other as conscious, given that consciousness as such is not empirically verifiable. Sartre denies that that certainty is derived from a *proof* of the existence of others, any more than Descartes' certainty about his own existence was derived from the *cogito* (*BN*, 251).[9] Since Sartre rejects the idea that the existence of others can be proved, the arguments he presents are apparently intended to support the claim that the immediate awareness we have of the other is what it seems to be. Since Sartre rejects the idea that the consciousness of others is empirically verifiable as such, our certainty of the existence of the other as conscious must ultimately rest on something other than sense observation.

The ground for certainty of the existence of others as conscious is "a primary relation between my consciousness and the other's" (*BN*, 253). There are two basic forms of relation to the other. It is not only possible for me to intend Peter as an object, which is the case just described, but it is also possible for Peter to intend me as an object. When this occurs, I am as certain of

8. Alvin Plantinga, *God and Other Minds: A Study of the Rational Justification of Belief in God* (Ithaca, N.Y.: Cornell University Press, 1967), p. 252.

9. Cf. Plantinga, *God and Other Minds*, pp. 268–69. Plantinga also denies that certainty of the existence of others rests on proof; the belief is rational, he says, although the proofs are unsatisfactory.

the other as I am of my own existence; it is in fact a discovery of my own existence, in one sense (*BN*, 285). For Sartre, the other's intending me as an object is a condition of my knowing my objective self and being able to apply certain kinds of predicates to myself in reflection; on a deeper level, it is the primary condition of my very existence as an object (*BN*, 280). It is important at this point to see the indirect manner of Sartre's approach to the problem of other minds.

The question of the existence of others has usually centered on the alleged difficulty of knowing whether the other is conscious; we can see the behavior of the other, but there is supposed to be a kind of gulf that separates his behavior from such experiences as pain. We saw that Sartre denied there is a problem of this kind, either theoretically or in our everyday experience. There is, on the other hand, another very real difficulty. The skeptic has usually assumed (without discussion) that we are certain of the assertion "I exist." Sartre points out that in one important sense of the ambiguous word "I," this is a problematic claim. The problem we really face is that our view of the world is from a certain perspective, and that we cannot look upon that perspective from the outside. Our visual perception of the world proceeds from a certain point on our body; we cannot, however, " 'see the seeing,' " Sartre says (*BN*, 304). The body is the center from which we see, but it is physically impossible for us to get an "outside look" at ourselves seeing the tree.

There is an analogous difficulty, however, with regard to all of our intentions. Sartre insists that this is the reason for the prevalence of a double standard (*BN*, 528). People frequently judge their own actions differently from those of others, not because they are deliberately deceitful but because they literally are unable to see their own actions and blame themselves in the same way they can see the actions of others and blame them. This, in fact, often gives rise to talk about unconscious intentions. There is a sense, of course, in which we can try to "take a look" at ourselves. We try to imagine what our actions and utterances would be like from the point of view of other people. How do we go about this? Sartre answers: "I have often grasped by intuition as regards others the nature of vulgarity; thus I can apply the word 'vulgar' to my person. But I cannot join the meaning of this word to my person" (*BN*, 527).

Initially, Sartre's first point appears to be quite similar to one made by Strawson, that a necessary condition of ascribing experiences and states of consciousness to oneself is that one has to be prepared to ascribe them to others.[10] Sartre is saying that a necessary condition of ascribing such predicates as "vulgar" to oneself is that one has been able to ascribe them to others. It should be noted, however, that the apparent similarity in approach conceals some important differences.

In the first place, Sartre is working with a very different type of predicate. That is, he sees the basic problem not as discovering whether the other is conscious but of discovering how we appear from the outside, given that we cannot ever really stand back from and look at ourselves. So the problematic predicates, as far as Sartre is concerned, are not those connected with others' states of consciousness but those which, when applied to ourselves, imply an "outside view" in either a literal or figurative sense. The character predicates are of this sort—for instance, "kind"—and such others as "ugly," or "handsome," or "vulgar."

Another important difference between Sartre and Strawson is that while both are concerned with the application of certain kinds of predicates, Sartre wishes to add an ontological claim to the linguistic point. That is, I am not and cannot be kind to myself; nor could I be kind to a stone. If I exist as a kind person, there must be some conscious object of kindness. Nor can I be ugly for myself, since I view the world from my body. If I am ugly, I can be ugly only for someone who views my body from his center of reference. This difference remains to be spelled out.

Even when we have learned to apply "outside view" predicates correctly to ourselves, Sartre says there is the further problem that we cannot "join the meaning of the word to my person." We can never really grasp the meaning of these predicates as applied to ourselves, any more than we can see what our eyes look like when they are seeing. It is at this point that an analogy *is* needed; we imagine our own body and behavior on the model of the other's body and behavior (*BN*, 354).

It remains a fact that, in spite of the difficulty, we can apply character predicates and other "outside view" predicates to ourselves; and we can do so in most cases correctly, even when we are unable to feel that correctness. We are able to reflect upon our own actions and utterances; we can thus discover objective patterns in our own past conduct, which is to say that we can take a semi-objective, semi-outside look at it. The importance for morality of the ability to reflect is obvious. But

10. *Individuals*, p. 94.

how can we account for this ability? Sartre's answer provides the key to his indirect account of how we can be certain of the existence of others. Reflection, he says, is "an abortive effort on the part of the for-itself *to be another* while *remaining itself*" (*BN*, 161). However, we can predicate qualities of ourselves only through the "objectifying power" of the other as mediator; it is, in other words, the other who "teaches me who I am" (*BN*, 274). Sartre admits that the point is not a new one, but claims that those who have defended this thesis become trapped in a vicious circle by deriving the concept of the other from an analogy with myself.

There are two ways that the other can perform his function as mediator. He can simply apply certain verbal predicates to my behavior, as I do to his, and in this way teach me who I am. He can also do this to me directly and nonverbally, by means of a look; in this case it is the existence of my objective self which is produced. In Sartre's example, I am absorbed in looking through a keyhole, and suddenly discover that my action is the object of someone else's gaze. "It is shame or pride which reveals to me the other's look and myself at the end of that look. It is the shame or pride which makes me *live*, not *know* the situation of being looked at" (*BN*, 261).

Sartre's argument can be paraphrased as follows:

1. No nonconscious existent can intend objects; only conscious existents can intend objects (*BN*, 257, 289).
2. I cannot intend my own intending as an object (*BN*, 298).
3. In certain types of experience (e.g., shame and pride), I discover that I have undergone a radical transformation from being a subject to being an object; that is, I discover that my intentional acts have been intended from a spatial and purposive point of reference, not my own (*BN*, 260–63).

Conclusion: I can exist as an object only if some conscious existent, other than myself, has made an object of my intending (*BN*, 257).

The point was made earlier, and should be reiterated, that Sartre does not think my certainty of the existence of others rests on proof; it rests, rather, on my mediate awareness of my objective self. His argument is apparently intended as support for saying that a necessary condition of my having an objective self, as well as becoming reflectively aware of that self, is that conscious others should have intended me as an object. Sartre's keyhole example is one that overemphasizes, perhaps, the moment of self-recognition that will form the basis for further reflective activity. It should be added that the described moment does not occur in a temporal vacuum, but presupposes a history of learning how the language is correctly applied in cases other than one's own.

Premise 1 simply restates the point discussed earlier, that conscious relations are intentional while nonconscious ones are not. Premise 2 is analogous to Ryle's saying he can point *with* his index finger and other people can point *at* it, but it can't itself be the object at which it is pointing.[11]

Premise 3 needs to be discussed further. A. J. Ayer objects to it by saying Sartre begs the question if he assumes that he really is the object of someone else's gaze. On the other hand, Sartre may be saying that he only thinks he is being observed, but this could be the case, Ayer insists, even if no one is actually observing him.[12]

Sartre agrees that we might be mistaken in thinking we see a real human being in the particular case he discusses; all of our sense knowledge is only probable, he insists. How, then, can he claim certainty about the existence of the other, when it appears to depend on our corrigible sense perception of someone else in the corridor? Sartre begins a reply by saying that while it is true that in this particular instance, or in any other single instance, I may be mistaken about there being a human person looking at me or speaking to me, I could not be mistaken in general about the existence of others who have intended me as an object (*BN*, 280–81).

Sartre bases this claim on the following point. When another intends me as an object, I am as certain of his existence as I am of my own existence, for the very good reason that it is in fact a discovery of my own existence insofar as I have an objective self—or self-for-others, as Sartre sometimes puts it (*BN*, 285). I cannot have a social self for myself. It is not possible that I could be ugly or witty or vulgar alone; if I lived in solitude, then I could not lie, snoop, or be kind, and the terms "liar," "peeping Tom," or "kind" would be inapplicable to my behavior. It is a form of existence of myself that comes into being, and a form of existence of myself that I discover, through the necessary mediation of the other, when he intends me as an object (*BN*, 271, 524).

11. Ryle, *Concept of Mind*, p. 197.
12. Ayer, "Novelist-Philosophers," p. 105.

One of the mistakes usually made in discussions of the existence of other minds, however, has been to assume that there is no problem connected with our certainty of the claim "I exist." Sartre has argued for the ambiguity of the concept of a person; and in one important sense of the word "I" there is such a problem, as he points out when he discusses the difficulty of taking an outside view of ourselves and the prevalence of the use of a double standard. Once it is shown how we can exist as objects, and how we can know that we have an objective existence, and thus take a reflective stance with regard to our own actions, an indirect answer to the problem of the existence of others has been given.

The point of the keyhole example is that my shame is a recognition of the truth of an outside appraisal of my behavior. At first I was only prereflectively aware of the keyhole, and of my purpose in looking through it. My red face is an implicit admission that I suddenly recognize my own action as the type to which I would apply the expression "snooping" if it were performed by another. My action has been altered from one performed solely for my own purpose into an action which also has an objective side; that is, the same action is suddenly seen in terms of another's goal of preserving his privacy. A purpose alien to my own has brought this objective character of my act into existence. Since my sense perception is corrigible, the other may really be there in the corridor, but he might not be. This would not make a difference in the particular case, since Sartre's point is that my existence as an object in relation to another's purposes, and my ability to reflect and to apply the character predicate the other would have applied if he had been present, can only be accounted for on the basis of others in my language community having been present at other times.

The answer to Ayer's criticism, which says that Sartre begs the question, is twofold. First, Sartre claims that it would be impossible in principle for us to exist as objects and as possessors of certain kinds of character traits except in relation to conscious others whose purposes run counter to our own. Second, it would be impossible in principle for us to use language in the way we do, to apply character predicates and other "outside view" predicates to ourselves and to our behavior, and to take a semi-objective viewpoint on ourselves in reflection unless we had observed others acting similarly and unless others had described our actions to us from their point of view (BN, 267, 373). "The other accomplishes for us a function of which we are incapable and which nevertheless is incumbent on us: *to see ourselves as we are*" (*BN*, 354). Without the mediation of the other, we would not be able to say "I" in reflective utterances. But we *can* do this. The question of the existence of others can be resolved in a general way, then, even though Sartre admits there may be a question in the particular case. This would be enough to refute the solipsist, if there were no further problems.

However, a further objection to Sartre's account of the existence of other minds is that if a single human being lived alone in a world in which there were mirrors, it would be possible to account for his use of "outside view" predicates by his mirrored view of himself. One would not need to assume, in this case, that other conscious beings exist. While the objection seems initially plausible, it does not hold up as a strong argument against Sartre's position. To begin with, general objections may be made to the notion that individuals could use language at all, or form concepts, in the absence of human society. There are, in addition, particular objections to the claim that we could use character predicates, and certain other kinds of relational predicates, in a world that did not include human speakers.

Sartre might ask how the critic proposed to derive the use of a word such as "kind" from a mirror image. The concept of kindness implies a relation between conscious beings who are in radically different situations: one of them, for instance, in a position to be helpful or compassionate, the other in a position of needing help or sympathy. If the solitary individual looks at his mirror image, what would he see—an individual wearing a compassionate facial expression? Perhaps. But unless this compassion were *directed toward* some being less fortunate than oneself, the use of the term "kind" would be a misapplication.

If, on the other hand, one looked in the mirror and saw not compassion but distress on the features of the mirror image, there would be, in this case also, insufficient reason for the correct application of the term "kind." The latter mirror image might at best give a reason for the use of a nonrelational predicate such as "in pain." But why would there be need for a mirror in this case?

There is, of course, at least one other possibility. One might look in the mirror and see a complete act of kindness performed between two people. The difficulty would be that, in this case, a second conscious being has been introduced into the mirror scene, and the mirror device would no longer serve as a *substitute* for other minds in the process of learning to apply character predicates. Similar problems would attend the attempt to use mirrors to explain other character predicates: "cruel" and "honest," for example.

Sartre could use a similar approach in some of the other "outside view" predicates which less obviously presuppose social relations. It might seem plausible to think of ugliness as simply a kind of irregular arrangement of features which might indeed be reflected by a mirror. Sartre has observed, however, that for a man, to be ugly is to have been rejected by many women. The obvious variety in cultural norms of beauty and ugliness also suggests the correctness of Sartre's claim that these are not intrinsic properties of the sort a mirror might reflect; rather, they are relational properties, applicable in a social context but not otherwise.

The critic's attempt to account for one's use of "outside view" predicates by mirrors does not seem to provide a real alternative to Sartre's claim that this can only be explained on the assumption that other conscious beings exist in relation to oneself.

An objection has been made that if we could be mistaken in the single instance, we could conceivably be mistaken every single time. Sartre is wrong in thinking that my ability to apply character and other "outside view" predicates to myself presupposes the existence of others; it actually requires only a *belief* in the existence of others. If this belief can be accounted for in some other way, such as my having grown up in a world of robots, then the belief might well be false and Sartre will be no better off than the skeptic.[13]

An initial reply might take the simple form of asking who programmed all those robots to perform this systematic deception? The programmer was no doubt a conscious being, as were the engineers who constructed these marvelous mechanisms. The fact that there are robots of the sort needed by the critic can only be accounted for on the assumption that there are other minds. But the critic had intended to eliminate all other conscious beings from the picture.

But let us take the critic's objection more seriously. If we look again at the example of the robot which had been programmed to search for library books, it is quite clear that such a robot, though it may exhibit something like purposive behavior, cannot perform the function of mediator which Sartre thinks other people do. Its purposes are too restricted and its responses

---

13. This objection was made by L. E. Sternberg.

are too limited. To see that this is so, we have only to ask what a world of robots would have to be like to account for the full range of character predicates and other "outside view" predicates for which Sartre wants to account.

Ayer has suggested that it would not be overly fanciful to imagine automata which could imitate human language and actions sufficiently to enable the child to learn to apply the concept of a person to himself, as well as to the robots.[14] But is this really so with regard to the type of claim Sartre is making? If we look at some common examples of character predicates, it becomes obvious that robots will not only have to feign speech but will also have to simulate all or most life processes, for Sartre's point is that an entire network of social concepts is involved in our reflective activity.

Am I a glutton? Well, no—not when I compare my eating habits to those of Henry and Mortimer (alias Robot H and Robot M?). Am I cruel? I would prefer not to think so, but when I was angry the other day I kicked Henry; and the big black and blue mark on his leg is still evident, though not as bad as it was two days ago. This morning I was playing with a knife; it slipped and cut Mortimer's finger, and instead of bolts and screws pouring out, it bled, just as my finger bleeds when it is cut. I know how to apply the predicate "murderer," even though I am not a murderer, because that term was applied when Joe killed Charlie (alias Robot J and Robot C?). I happened to come upon the murder scene, unfortunately, and I can distinguish murdering someone from simply destroying a machine. The critic has to assume that a robot can be constructed whose inner workings resemble organs, bones, etc.— rather than wires and batteries—in appearance and operation, so that the "murdered" robot can make a convincingly gory corpse.

How are we to understand those predicates connected with parent-child relationships, and how can I learn to apply them to myself? Am I a good parent? Which of these robots is the mother or father of my child? Did I enjoy conceiving the child? (Would you want your daughter to marry a robot?) Is the child itself half-human, half-robot? Does a half-human, half-robot child count as another mind? Does my child grow as fast as your child? If I am to be able to apply such relational predicates as "frigid," "homosexual," "slut," "Don Juan," etc., to myself,

14. A. J. Ayer, *Concept of a Person and Other Essays* (New York: St. Martin's Press, 1963), p. 107.

it is only on the assumption that the robots perform sexual acts in a variety of ways, and that I can understand how my own responses resemble or differ from theirs.

The robots must not only eat, engage in sexual relations, grow, etc., but they must exhibit a high level of intelligence in a variety of ways. Let us say that I know how to apply the relational predicate "excellent surgeon" to my own case, which presupposes that I have performed successful operations on my patients to restore their health. I am an excellent doctor in relation to (a) patients whose pains I have banished and whose anxieties I have calmed and (b) a body of research about physical and psychosomatic illnesses. Although I did not perform this research, I have mastered the results of others' research in the field of my specialty. (c) And I am excellent in relation to other doctors, whose skill or knowledge or sensitivity is somewhat less than my own. The critic must assume that patients, researchers, and other doctors are all highly complicated robots.

Again, I can sit in my room and write, but I can also more or less correctly apply the terms "good writer" or "hack writer" to myself. Sartre would say this presupposes that I have been able to examine the writings of others and have had the deficiencies in my own writings pointed out. The critic is supposing that the really fine robot poet has been able, without possessing consciousness, to write movingly about sunsets and lost lovers.

The critic must assume that the town drunk, who undergoes a religious conversion and becomes, overnight, a solid citizen, is a robot whose mechanism is complicated enough to have been designed for two quite different purposes. In the case of the Southern white robot who persecutes blacks, then undergoes a change of "heart" and becomes the defender of blacks, the assumption must be made that the robot has been designed to fulfill opposite purposes.

And so on. Examples could be multiplied endlessly, but the point is no doubt clear. A very large number of predicates can be counted among the character predicates or relational "outside view" predicates. The critic must in fact make the assumption that his robots can do everything people can do in order to account for the full range of "outside view" and character predicates which in fact we have, and which in fact we can apply to our own character and conduct.

The critic has claimed that someone brought up among robots might conceivably be mistaken every single time about whether a conscious being intended him as an object. He has said that the belief in the existence of others is all that is needed, but that this belief might actually be false. Whether it is conceivable that someone could be mistaken every single time depends, I think, on whether it is conceivable that robots can not only search for library books—which is what one kind is built to do—but can eat, bleed, grow, mate, bear children, laugh, cry, murder, do research, write sensitive and moving poems, be sick, heal the sick, and build other robots which can search for library books.

But let me add an even more damaging example. To simulate the full range of human activities, the deceived person will have to be able to distinguish robots from nonrobots. To do this he must be able to tell what persons can do and what robots cannot do. In addition to the vital and conscious activities mentioned, persons can make their own rules and set their own goals, and can sometimes break all the rules they know. When confronted with conflicting rules, such as a self-regarding rule and a moral rule, human beings are capable of moral autonomy in the sense that they may consider those rules and choose between them. But robots can only follow instructions. Even if the instructions are very complex, the robot differs from the person in that the robot cannot make its own rules or choose its own goals or violate all of its instructions. If two conflicting instructions are given the robot, it proceeds to follow whichever one is given first.

Thus if the deceived person cannot tell the difference between himself and the robots which surround him, he lacks one kind of concept that we in fact possess. If the deceived person can tell the difference between himself and these programmed machines, one must ask what unprogrammed creatures showed him examples of autonomy with respect to rules. And one must ask the reason for denying such unprogrammed beings are persons and for claiming they are robots.

There is one other objection to Sartre's account, however, which may be difficult to answer. Sartre maintains, on the basis of some of the foregoing considerations, that I am as certain of the existence of the other as I am of my own (objective) existence since, in the objective sense of "I," my existence depends on there being another who has intended me as an object. The careful critic will have noticed that Sartre always suggests a certain degree of uneasiness about my knowledge of my objective self. In fact, it is because I am to some degree uncertain that I tend to apply a double standard, etc. The critic may ask whether Sartre isn't simply adding a new form of skepticism, rather than answering the skeptic. Couldn't Sartre's argument be taken simply as showing that we are less than fully certain about the existence of others? All he has done, perhaps, is show that we have equally certain knowledge in both cases but not complete certainty in either case.

I am not sure that the following reply does full justice to the criticism, but it may do so—it depends, I think, on what type of uncertainty Sartre is dealing with. Sartre has said that we know how to apply the term "vulgar" to ourselves but that we cannot "join the meaning" of the term to ourselves. It is not entirely clear what he means by this, but perhaps the following suggestion is a plausible interpretation. Isn't the problem that we all prefer to think well of ourselves, and that we do not easily accept uncomplimentary epithets applied to our behavior, even though we are all perfectly capable of knowing (in a way different but no less certain than others know) what action we have performed? This interpretation can be supported by noticing that Sartre uses uncomplimentary adjectives as examples in discussing the double-standard cases. But perhaps we would have much less difficulty in "joining the meaning" of the word "kind" to ourselves. If this is a correct interpretation, the uncertainty he refers to is merely a psychological, not an epistemological, uncertainty and hence is irrelevant to the problem. The philosophical question of the knowledge of other minds can be given an indirect resolution, then, even though some psychological uncertainty remains.

That psychological uncertainty is surely connected with our wish not to know the worst about ourselves, and thus we can see one main point of Sartre's substitution of the prereflective/reflective distinction for Freud's unconscious mind. According to Sartre, we usually perform actions prereflectively in accord with our own purposes, without stopping to reflect on the sometimes uncomfortable point that those actions may appear very different to others who have different purposes. While Freud would perhaps bring in the complicated mechanism of an unconscious mind, and unverifiable hypotheses about a primal scene to account for the keyhole example, for Sartre there is no question of the snooper's being unconscious of what he is doing. He has simply failed (until surprised) to draw the connection between his lived action and that same act as it would be viewed by another, or by himself if he were to take an objective look at his behavior. It is a somewhat different case when there has been a whole series of similar past actions. What Freud would call an unconscious tendency to snoop is described by

Sartre as a refusal in bad faith to reflect on the pattern of actions unreflectively performed. The point of existential therapy is to bring the patient to a reflective recognition of the objective claims that other persons can make with respect to the patient's action patterns.

Chapter 7

Concluding Remarks

Sartre's concept of the person as moral agent has been discussed in connection with issues that have been raised by contemporary analytic philosophers. On the basis of this study, Sartre's concept of the person can be said to be fundamentally coherent, and can be compared favorably with positions defended by many contemporary English-speaking philosophers.

Sartre's analysis is not without faults, although it has been shown that some of the more common criticisms, such as the alleged misuse of *"néant"* as a substantive, rest on a misunderstanding of Sartre's position. At various points I have distinguished between Sartre's overstated claims and the actual positions he defends. His real claims are often sounder and more interesting than the inflated slogan forms would suggest. Thus, while he sometimes speaks sweepingly of "total freedom," I have argued that Sartre is actually defending a view of the choice of ideal self, and that his doctrine bears some surprising resemblances to B. F. Skinner's actual but unannounced position. Sartre is clearly guilty of misleading us, however, or perhaps jesting, when he introduces jargon and slogans.

Most of the other faults that have been identified in this study are due to Sartre's failure to carry some of his positions to full clarity. The problem in these cases is incompleteness, rather than incoherence. The most serious gap in Sartre's account pertains to his key concept of choice: he offers no way of distinguishing between a series of actions resulting from some physiological abnormality and those series of acts which normal people perform in the attempt to bring about their chosen ends. Problems with Sartre's Summary Theory of character were also discussed, and it was suggested that Sartre's frequency view needs to be supplemented with certain kinds of qualitative considerations.

It was noted that Sartre describes, but does not attempt to provide a metaphysical explanation for, the "irreducibility" of consciousness to physical phenomena. There are a few elements within Sartre's position which suggest, however, that what he really needs, and is probably heading toward, is a form of physicalism that is broad enough to include the intentional properties of consciousness. Jerome Shaffer has made the interesting suggestion that the mind-body problem would be much closer to a solution if it turned out that we had privileged access to some physical events.[1]

Sartre has denied the need for any subject other than the body. Furthermore, in his insistence that the body-subject has privileged access to many of its own states, physical positions, and acts, Sartre undercuts the important and prevalent notion that the asymmetry of first- and third-person statements represents a dichotomy between mental and physical substances. Sartre, clearly, has not taken us all the way home, but his early work pointed in the direction of a possible resolution, and his more recent work, still metaphysically wary, takes us considerably farther in the same direction.

Sartre's concept of the person has some additional strengths. One is that his discussion of criteria of personal identity permits him to defend a view of the person as an accountable moral agent, which seems to be very close to what we actually use and require. Sartre's claim that bodily identity is a necessary condition of personal identity in the strong sense (as opposed to the weak sense, defended by Strawson) is an assumption we need if we are to defend our present methods of locating and punishing guilty persons and proving the innocence of others after a time interval.[2]

One of the most interesting moral applications of Sartre's concept of a person is in his account of bad faith or self-deception. This is intended to be an alternative to a Freudian view of self-deception based on the notion of an unconscious

1. Jerome Shaffer, "Recent Work on the Mind-Body Problem," *American Philosophical Quarterly*, 2, no. 2 (April 1965): 84, 98.
2. If it is indeed the case that the notion of moral accountability presupposes the claim that bodily identity is a necessary condition of personal identity, then one consequence seems to be that there is a lack of coherence in our ordinary ideas about persons. Discussion of souls or persons has generally taken place in the context of two different kinds of questions: we have discussed persons as moral agents who could perform actions for which they are held responsible, but we have also been concerned about the question of immortality. Our tradition has probably not distinguished sharply enough between the kind of concept of the person needed in a moral context and the kind of idea that makes sense within a religious context. To the extent that the idea of immortality rests on the assumption that body and person are separable, it may be that a choice must be made between a moral and a religious concept of the person.

mind; it is based on Sartre's claim that there are different uses of the term "I" and on his distinction between the prereflective and reflective levels of consciousness. To be in bad faith is to refuse responsibility for ourselves, Sartre says. But since there are different aspects of the self, there are different ways of refusing it.

For instance, we can try to believe that our character (past series of actions) prohibits us from making some present choice, or we might be in bad faith by claiming, as Garcin did in *No Exit*, that the future ideal self is the only true self, regardless of how little our past actions tended in that direction.

So long as we engage in our actions prereflectively, we can try to ignore the objective self we always present to others, and to ourselves when we reflect. Only when we are willing to reflect on ourselves objectively enough to see the patterns of our past actions and the real connections between what we are, have been, and want to be can we hope to assume genuine responsibility for ourselves.

Sartre's discussion of the objective and interpretive elements in remembering was directed especially to the problem of how we can conceive of persons as accountable in relation to past events which are sometimes assumed to render persons non-responsible for their present actions.

Sartre's discussion of character, conceived as the basic pattern of past actions, is again close to what is required in our moral judgments. Character, viewed as something more than this pattern of actions, appeared to be both mysterious and unnecessary, since the body-subject itself acts. Sartre's position allows for uncharacteristic actions, and also for change of character, as we understand these—for instance, in our excuse and parole procedures.

Insofar as the choice of fundamental project is seen as a selection of an ideal self, along with a corresponding world view, Sartre's position could be compared to that of R. M. Hare, who suggests that in one's choice of moral ideals one is treating one's character and one's life as an art work.[3] While Sartre stresses that there are no interproject reasons which might be used to justify that fundamental choice of project, he does not describe the choice as capricious but rather as one that is intended to make sense out of a number of givens (past, biological makeup, objective elements in the situation, etc.).

3. R. M. Hare, *Freedom and Reason* (New York: Oxford University Press, 1965), p. 150.

If Sartre departs from our ordinary view of moral agents, that departure is to be found in his insistence that the ideal self, in terms of which we are able to present reasons for our acts, may be what the moral philosopher or the ordinary person would consider bad, as in the case of Jean Genet's choice to be a thief. There are no common nonbiological human ends, and no universal moral ideals, which pose a limit to the kind of fundamental project which can be chosen. It is with respect to the radical pluralism of ideals, but probably not before this, that the moral philosopher might argue that Sartre has abandoned the ordinary idea of an accountable moral agent.

Two types of consideration make me hesitate about accepting this point. First, I am not fully persuaded that Sartre would defend the position that there are no moral limits whatsoever to the type of end which might be chosen, although these limits may be formal rather than substantial. There is a philosophical tradition which claims that inner harmony can only be reconciled with the choice of what is good. Whether Sartre would agree with Plato and Kierkegaard depends on whether he thinks the coherence and continuity which are the ultimate point of anyone's choice of fundamental project are compatible with the most vicious ends.

In his play *The Devil and the Good Lord*, Sartre has one of his characters attempt to choose evil for the sake of evil. While one of the points Sartre makes in this play is that the man who acts solely on the basis of so-called "good principles" may be as destructive of human life as the man who acts solely on an evil principle, it is clear that he is criticizing wanton destruction on either ground. Furthermore, he has one of the supporting characters point out that the result of choosing pure evil is chaos.

There is additional support for this point in Sartre's popular essay "Existentialism Is a Humanism" and in Simone de Beauvoir's *The Ethics of Ambiguity*, both of which suggest the need for a formal, if not a substantive, moral limit to what Sartre thinks may be chosen as an end by the person who seeks unity. This is offered as a guess, however, rather than as an assertion, for Sartre often seems to be more anxious to emphasize the plurality of possible ideal selves than the limits.

The second reason for hesitation is that when we speak of a "moral agent," we surely do not intend to say that all of his actions and beliefs are morally good. Rather, in calling him a "moral agent" we want to call attention to the fact that this person is responsible for acting in whatever way he does. I am not a moral agent with respect to a storm that blows my ship off course, but I am a moral agent—that is, accountable—with respect to my act of steering the boat into the rocks. That is, to be a moral agent does not presuppose that one is a morally *good* agent. Sartre's pluralism of ideals assumes complete moral freedom of choice of ideals; and this may not be as far from the ordinary view of the moral agent as it first appears.

From the point of view of most English-speaking philosophers, one of the most obvious advantages of Sartre's concept of a person is that it is very economical. His one-substance view of persons does not require him to posit a variety of unnecessary entities. He has argued against the need for intentional objects immanent in consciousness. He claimed that the concept of a person is ambiguous; the ability to say "I" when the body is not being referred to can be accounted for by an additional reflective act of the body-subject. No additional immaterial subject is needed.

Sartre accounts for the continuity and coherence of actions and utterances by arguing, in part, that there is a single, fundamental end for each person at any given time, which is the organizing principle that permits integration of his actions and utterances. Many "I" statements refer to the system of conscious relations, or to parts of this system, which is organized by reference to the ideal project. Sartre compares his own view to that of the classical theorists and says that while they are correct in thinking each human organism refers to something beyond what we can perceive of it, their mistake is to think that that unperceived something must be an immaterial substance or a Kantian noumenal self (*BN*, 253). Sartre's economy is to try to account for most of the same phenomena by positing only one existent substance and one nonexistent self—a body-subject and an ideal self—which gives point to a series of acts of the body-subject.

Not everyone is happy with Sartre's appeal to Occam's razor. One of the main themes of the phenomenological movement, in fact, has been its antireductionism. Sartre has been criticized for his refusal to remain within the spirit of the orthodox phenomenological movement, while claiming that his own work is phenomenological.[4]

It would take us beyond the scope of this study to attempt to trace the exact points at which Sartre agrees and disagrees

---

4. Herbert Spiegelberg has taken Sartre to task for his use of Occam's razor. See his "Husserl's Phenomenology and Existentialism," *Journal of Philosophy*, 57, no. 2 (January 1960): 71.

with his colleagues in the phenomenological movement; however, our discussion might permit the following initial reply to this particular criticism. It is at least possible that Sartre's discussion of the ambiguity of the concept of the person may be read in the antireductionist spirit of the phenomenological movement. That is, he may have intended in this way to retain the descriptive complexity of a phenomenological approach while attempting to combine it with an ontological simplicity. Whether this would reconcile him to his critics is another question.

Sartre has been criticized more than once for his lack of originality, and a number of writers have discussed his ideas in relation to those of Husserl, Heidegger, and Hegel.[5] There seems to be little question that Sartre's early existentialist writings are eclectic, although the point has hardly been mentioned in the present study. The line of approach we have followed has been to exhibit the basic coherence of the concept of a person which Sartre has pieced together, without attempting to determine the extent of his originality. One reason he has been able to achieve this coherence, perhaps, is that he has used a few relatively simple concepts to account for a wide variety of phenomena.

One example of this is his use of the concept of intentionality. He takes a simple idea: that consciousness refers, that it can refer to a variety of nonexistent objects or states of affairs. Add, for each human being, one particular nonexistent object, the ideal self. Sartre is able to use this simple basis in his accounts of such widely differing phenomena as human rationality, our awareness of the existence of other persons, and certain forms of dislocation in memory, as when we remember something as if it had happened to another person.

In addition to showing the basic coherence of Sartre's early concept of a person, this study has attempted to show that Sartre's discussion is addressed to certain familiar questions,

---

5. The reader who is interested in tracing out some of the historical connections might look at Spiegelberg's The Phenomenological Movement; a brief study of some of these connections is also given in Spiegelberg's article "Husserl's Phenomenology and Existentialism." Also see Mary Warnock, The Philosophy of Sartre; Klaus Hartmann, Sartre's Ontology (Evanston, Ill.: Northwestern University Press, 1966); Jean Wahl, A Short History of Existentialism (New York: Wisdom Library, 1949); Alfred Schuetz, "Sartre's Theory of the Alter Ego," Philosophy and Phenomenological Research, 9, no. 2 (December 1948): 181–99; and Herbert Marcuse, "Existentialism: Remarks on Jean-Paul Sartre's L'Etre et le Néant," Philosophy and Phenomenological Research, 8, no. 3 (March 1948): 309–36.

such as how we know that other conscious minds exist, whether language about conscious phenomena can be reduced to talk about physical objects, whether it is logically possible for persons to exist apart from their bodies, and whether "I" refers ambiguously.

I believe the present study has shown even more, however. The concept of a person to be found in Sartre's early work is not only intelligible but significant. He has led us away from some of the idle considerations in much contemporary analytic discussion of persons *qua* perceivers and has offered important and probably correct solutions to some of the most pressing and central problems connected with persons considered as moral agents.

Selected Bibliography

Works by Sartre

Sartre, Jean-Paul. *The Age of Reason*. Translated by Eric Sutton. New York: Bantam Books, 1959.

———. *Baudelaire*. Translated by Martin Turnell. New York: New Directions Publishing Corp., 1950.

———. *Being and Nothingness: An Essay on Phenomenological Ontology*. Translated by Hazel E. Barnes. New York: Philosophical Library, 1956.

———. *The Condemned of Altona*. Translated by Sylvia and George Leeson. Introduction by Henri Peyre. New York: Alfred A. Knopf, 1961.

———. *The Devil and the Good Lord and Two Other Plays*. Translated by Kitty Black, Sylvia Leeson, and George Leeson. New York: Random House, 1960.

———. *The Emotions: Outline of a Theory*. Translated by Bernard Frechtman. New York: Philosophical Library, 1948.

———. "Existentialism Is a Humanism." Translated by Philip Mairet. In *Existentialism from Dostoevsky to Sartre*. Edited by Walter Kaufmann. New York: Meridian Books, 1957.

———. "Une idée fondamentale de la phénoménologie de Husserl: l'intentionnalité." *Situations* I. Paris: Gallimard, 1947. Joseph Fell's translation of this article appears in *Journal of the British Society for Phenomenology*, 1, no. 2 (May 1970): 4–5.

———. *Imagination: A Psychological Critique*. Translated by Forrest Williams. Ann Arbor, Mich.: University of Michigan Press, 1962.

———. "Interview with Sartre." *New York Review of Books*, March 26, 1970, pp. 22–31 (world copyright, *New Left Review*).

———. *Intimacy and Other Stories*. Translated by Lloyd Alexander. Norfolk, Conn.: New Directions, 1948.

———. "Materialism and Revolution." *Literary and Philosophical Essays*. Translated by Annette Michelson. New York: Collier Books, 1962.

——— *Nausea*. Translated by Lloyd Alexander. Norfolk, Conn.: New Directions, 1949.

———. "No Exit." Translated by Stuart Gilbert. *No Exit and Three Other Plays*. New York: Random House, 1946.

——— *The Psychology of the Imagination*. New York: Citadel Press, 1948.

——— *The Reprieve*. Translated by Eric Sutton. New York: Bantam Books, 1960.

———. *Saint Genet: Actor and Martyr*. Translated by Bernard Frechtman. New York: New American Library, 1963.

———. *The Transcendence of the Ego: An Existentialist Theory of Consciousness*. Translated by Forrest Williams and Robert Kirkpatrick. New York: Noonday Press, 1957.

———. *Troubled Sleep*. Translated by Gerard Hopkins. New York: Alfred A. Knopf, 1951.

———. *The Words*. Translated by Bernard Frechtman. New York: Fawcett World Library, 1966.

Works about Sartre

Abel, L. "Retroactive 'I.' " *Partisan Review*, 32 (Spring 1965): 255–61.

Albéres, René Marill [pseudonym]. *Jean-Paul Sartre: Philosopher without Faith*. Translated by Wade Baskin. New York: Philosophical Library, 1961.

Ames, Van Meter. "Fetichism in the Existentialism of Sartre." *Journal of Philosophy*, 47 (July 6, 1950):407–11.

———. "Mead and Sartre on Man." *Journal of Philosophy*, 53 (March 15, 1956):205–19.

Aron, R. "Sartre's Marxism." Translated by J. Weightman. *Encounter*, 24 (June 1965): 34–39.

Ayer, A. J. "Novelist-Philosophers: V—Jean-Paul Sartre." *Horizon*, 12 (1945): 12–26, 101–10.

Barnes, Hazel. *Sartre*. London: Quartet Books, 1974.

Barrett, William. *Irrational Man: A Study in Existential Philosophy*. Garden City, N.Y.: Doubleday, 1962.

Beauvoir, Simone de. *The Ethics of Ambiguity*. Translated by Bernard Frechtman. New York: Citadel Press, 1964.

———. *Force of Circumstance*. Translated by Richard Howard. New York: G.P. Putnam's Sons, 1964.

———. "Merleau-Ponty et le pseudo-Sartrisme." *Les Temps Modernes*, 10 (1955): 2072–2122.

Bergmann, Frithjof. "Sartre's Account of Self-Deception." Unpublished paper.

Boorsch, Jean. "Sartre's View of Cartesian Liberty." *Yale French Studies*, 1 (Spring–Summer 1948): 90–96.

Breisach, Ernst. *Introduction to Modern Existentialism*. New York: Grove Press, 1962.

Brown, S. M., Jr. "Atheistic Existentialism of Jean-Paul Sartre." *Philosophical Review*, 57 (March 1948): 158–66.

Burkle, H. R. "Schaff and Sartre on the Grounds of Individual Freedom." *International Philosophical Quarterly*, 5 (December 1965): 647–65.

Butts, R. E. "Does Intentionality Imply Being? A Paralogism in Sartre's Ontology." *Journal of Philosophy*, 55 (October 9, 1958): 911–12.

Champigny, Robert. *Stages on Sartre's Way, 1938–1952*. Bloomington: Indiana University Press, 1959.

Chiaromonte, N. "Sartre and the Prize." Translated by M. McCarthy. *Encounter*, 24 (February 1965): 55–57.

Coates, J. B. "Existentialist Ethics." *Fortnightly*, 181 (May 1954): 338–44.

Conkling, Mark. "Sartre's Refutation of the Freudian Unconscious." *Review of Existential Psychology and Psychiatry*, 8 (Spring 1968): 86–101.

Cranston, Maurice. *Jean-Paul Sartre*. New York: Grove Press, 1962.

Desan, Wilfred. *The Marxism of Jean-Paul Sartre*. Garden City, N.Y.: Doubleday, 1965.

_____. *The Tragic Finale: An Essay on the Philosophy of Jean-Paul Sartre*. Rev. ed. New York: Harper & Row, 1960.

Earle, William. "Man as the Impossibility of God." *Christianity and Existentialism: Essays by William Earle, James M. Edie and John Wild*. Evanston, Ill.: Northwestern University Press, 1963.

Fell, Joseph P., III. *Emotion in the Thought of Sartre*. New York and London: Columbia University Press, 1965.

_____. "Sartre's Theory of Motivation: Some Clarifications." *Journal of the British Society for Phenomenology*, 1, no. 2 (May 1970). 27–34.

Greene, Norman N. *Jean-Paul Sartre: The Existentialist Ethic*. Ann Arbor: University of Michigan Press, 1963.

Grene, Marjorie. "Sartre's Theory of the Emotions." *Yale French Studies*, 1 (Spring–Summer 1948): 97–101.

_____. *Sartre*. New York: New Viewpoints, 1973.

Jeanson, Francis. *Le Problème Moral et la Pensée de Sartre*. Lettre-préface de Jean-Paul Sartre. Paris: Editions du Seuil, 1965.

Journal of the British Society for Phenomenology, vol. 1, no. 2 (May 1970). This issue is dedicated to Sartre.

Kern, Edith, ed. *Sartre: A Collection of Critical Essays*. Englewood Cliffs, N.J.: Prentice-Hall, 1962.

Laing, Ronald David, and D. G. Cooper. *Reason and Violence: A Decade of Sartre's Philosophy, 1950–1960*. Foreword by J.-P. Sartre. New York: Humanities Press, 1964.

Manser, Anthony. *Sartre: A Philosophic Study*. London: Athlone Press for the University of London, 1966.

Marcuse, Herbert. "Existentialism: Remarks on Jean-Paul Sartre's *L'Être et le Néant*." *Philosophy and Phenomenological Research*, 8, no. 3 (March 1948): 309–36.

Murdoch, Iris. *Sartre: Romantic Rationalist*. New Haven, Conn.: Yale University Press, 1953.

Naess, Arne. *Four Modern Philosophers: Carnap, Wittgenstein, Heidegger, Sartre*. Translated by Alastair Hannay. Chicago and London: University of Chicago Press, 1968.

Natanson, Maurice Alexander. *A Critique of Jean-Paul Sartre's Ontology*. Lincoln, Neb.: University Press, 1951.

Newman, Fred. "The Origins of Sartre's Existentialism." *Ethics*, 76 (April 1966): 178–90.

Olafson, Frederick A. *Principles and Persons: An Ethical Interpretation of Existentialism*. Baltimore: The Johns Hopkins Press, 1967.

Olson, R. G. "Three Theories of Motivation in the Philosophy of Jean-Paul Sartre." *Ethics*, 66 (April 1956): 176–87.

Plantinga, Alvin C. "An Existentialist's Ethics." *Review of Metaphysics*, 12 (December 1958): 235–56.

Rau, C. "Ethical Theory of Jean-Paul Sartre." *Journal of Philosophy*, 46 (August 18, 1949): 536–45.

Salvan, Jacques Léon. *To Be and Not to Be: An Analysis of Jean-Paul Sartre's Ontology*. Detroit: Wayne State University Press, 1962.

Scanlon, John D. "Consciousness, the Streetcar, and the Ego: *Pro* Husserl, *Contra* Sartre." *Philosophical Forum*, no. 2 (Spring 1971).

Schaff, Adam. *A Philosophy of Man*. New York: Monthly Review Press, 1963.

Schuetz, Alfred. "Sartre's Theory of the Alter Ego." *Philosophy and Phenomenological Research*, 9, no. 2 (December 1948): 181–99.

Smith, Colin. *Contemporary French Philosophy: A Study in Norms and Values*. New York: Barnes & Noble, 1964.

Spiegelberg, Herbert. "Husserl's Phenomenology and Existentialism." *Journal of Philosophy*, 57, no. 2 (January 21, 1960): 62–74.

———. *The Phenomenological Movement: A Historical Introduction*. 2d ed., 2 vols. The Hague: Martinus Nijhoff, 1969.

Stern, Alfred. *Sartre, his Philosophy and Psychoanalysis*. New York: Liberal Arts Press, 1953.

Thody, Philip. *Jean-Paul Sartre: A Literary and Political Study*. London: Hamish Hamilton, 1960.

Warnock, Mary. *Ethics since 1900*. London: Oxford University Press, 1960.

———. *The Philosophy of Sartre*. New York: Barnes & Noble, 1965.

Zuidema, Syste Ulbe. *Sartre*. Translated by Dirk Jellema. Philadelphia: Presbyterian and Reformed Publishing Co., 1960.

Works on Philosophy of Mind and Related Issues in Ethics

Anderson, John. "The Non-existence of Consciousness." *Australasian Journal of Psychology* (1929), pp. 68–73.

Aquila, Richard E. "The Status of Intentional Objects." *New Scholasticism*, 45, no. 3 (Summer 1971): 427–56.

Aristotle. *Nicomachean Ethics*. The Basic Works of Aristotle. Edited by Richard McKeon. New York: Random House, 1941.

Armstrong, D. M. *A Materialist Theory of Mind*. London: Routledge & Kegan Paul; New York: Humanities Press, 1968.

Aune, Bruce. "Intention." *Encyclopedia of Philosophy*. Vol 4.

Austin, J. L. "Other Minds." *Logic and Language: Second Series*. Edited by Antony Flew. Garden City, N.Y.: Doubleday, 1965.

Ayer, A. J. *Concept of a Person and Other Essays*. New York: St. Martin's Press, 1963.

Benjamin, B. S. "Remembering." *Essays in Philosophical Psychology*. Edited by Donald F. Gustafson. Garden City, N.Y.: Doubleday, 1964.

Berofsky, Bernard, ed. *Free Will and Determinism*. New York and London: Harper & Row, 1966.

Boden, Margaret A. "Intentionality and Physical Systems." *Philosophy of Science*, 37, no. 2 (June 1970): 200–214.

Brandt, Richard B. "Blameworthiness and Obligation." *Essays in Moral Philosophy*. Edited by A. I. Melden. Seattle: University of Washington Press, 1958.

———. "Traits of Character: A Conceptual Analysis." *American Philosophical Quarterly*, 7, no. 1 (January 1970): 23–37.

———.and Jaegwon Kim. "Wants as Explanations of Actions." *Journal of Philosophy*, 60, no. 15 (July 18, 1963), 425–35.

Butler, Joseph. "On Personal Identity." *Body, Mind, and Death.* Edited by Antony Flew. Problems of Philosophy Series. New York: Macmillan, 1964; London: Collier-Macmillan, 1964.

Cameron, Norman. *Personality Development and Psychopathology: A Dynamic Approach.* Boston: Houghton Mifflin, 1963.

Campbell, C. A. "In Defence of Free Will." *In Defence of Free Will, with Other Philosophical Essays.* London: George Allen & Unwin, 1967.

———. *On Selfhood and Godhood.* London: George Allen & Unwin, 1957; New York: Macmillan, 1957.

Castañeda, Hector-Neri. "Consciousness and Behavior: Their Basic Connections." *Intentionality, Minds, and Perception.* Edited by Hector-Neri Castañeda. Detroit: Wayne State University Press, 1967.

Chisholm, Roderick M. "Brentano on Descriptive Psychology and the Intentional." *Phenomenology and Existentialism.* Edited by Edward N. Lee and Maurice Mandelbaum. Baltimore: The Johns Hopkins Press, 1967.

———. "Chisholm-Sellars Correspondence on Intentionality." *Minnesota Studies in the Philosophy of Science.* Vol. 2: *Concepts, Theories, and the Mind-Body Problem.* Edited by Herbert Feigl, Michael Scriven, and Grover Maxwell. Minneapolis: University of Minnesota Press, 1958.

———. "Intentionality." *Encyclopedia of Philosophy.* Vol. 4.

———. "On the Observability of the Self." *Philosophy and Phenomenological Research,* 30, no. 1 (September 1969): 7–21.

———. *Perceiving: A Philosophical Study.* Ithaca, N.Y.: Cornell University Press, 1957.

———. ed. *Realism and the Background of Phenomenology.* New York: The Free Press, 1960; London: Collier-Macmillan, 1960.

———. "Sentences about Believing." *Minnesota Studies in the Philosophy of Science.* Vol. 2: *Concepts, Theories, and the Mind-Body Problem.* Edited by Herbert Feigl, Michael Scriven, and Grover Maxwell. Minneapolis: University of Minnesota Press, 1958.

———. "On Some Psychological Concepts and the 'Logic' of Intentionality." *Intentionality, Minds, and Perception.* Edited by Hector-Neri Castañeda. Detroit: Wayne State University Press, 1967.

Cornman, James W. "Intentionality and Intensionality." *Philosophical Quarterly* (January 1962), pp. 44–52.

Deely, John N. "Ontological Status of Intentionality." *New Scholasticism,* 46, no. 2 (Spring 1972): 220–33.

Dennett, D. C. "Intentional Systems." *Journal of Philosophy,* 68, no. 4 (February 25, 1971): 87–106.

———. *Content and Consciousness.* London: Routledge & Kegan Paul; New York: Humanities Press, 1969.

Dewey, John. "The Vanishing Subject in the Psychology of James." *Journal of Philosophy,* 37, no. 22 (October 24, 1940), 589–99.

Edwards, Paul. "Hard and Soft Determinism." *Determinism and Freedom in the Age of Modern Science.* Edited by Sidney Hook. New York: Collier Books, 1961.

Feigl, Herbert. "The 'Mental' and the 'Physical.' " *Minnesota Studies in the Philosophy of Science.* Vol. 2: *Concepts, Theories, and the Mind-Body Problem.* Edited by Herbert Feigl, Michael Scriven, and Grover Maxwell. Minneapolis: University of Minnesota Press, 1958.

Flew, Antony. "The Question of Survival." *Religious Belief and Philosophical Thought.* Edited by William P. Alston. New York: Harcourt, Brace & World, 1963.

Frankfurt, Harry G. "Freedom of the Will and the Concept of a Person." *Journal of Philosophy,* 68, no. 1 (January 14, 1971): 5–20.

Grice, H. P. "Personal Identity." *Mind,* 50 (October 1941): 330–50.

Grossman, Reinhardt. "Acts and Relations in Brentano." *Analysis,* 21, no. 1 (October 1960): 1–5.

Gurwitsch, Aron. "A Non-egological Conception of Consciousness." *Philosophy and Phenomenological Research,* 1 (March 1941): 325–38.

———. "Towards a Theory of Intentionality." *Philosophy and Phenomenological Research,* 30, no. 3 (March 1970): 354–67.

Hampshire, Stuart. "Dispositions." *Analysis,* 14 (1953): 5–11.

———. *Thought and Action.* New York: Viking Press, 1960.

Hardie, W. F. R. "The Final Good in Aristotle's *Ethics.*" *Aristotle: A Collection of Critical Essays.* Edited by J. M. E. Moravcsik. Garden City, N.Y.: Doubleday, 1967.

Hare, R. M. *Freedom and Reason.* New York: Oxford University Press, 1965.

———. *The Language of Morals.* New York: Oxford University Press, 1964.

Heidelberger, Herbert. "On Characterizing the Psychological." *Philosophy and Phenomenological Research,* 26, no. 4 (June 1966): 529–36.

Hospers, John. *Human Conduct: An Introduction to the Problems of Ethics.* New York: Harcourt, Brace & World, 1961.

———. "What Means This Freedom?" *Determinism and Freedom in the Age of Modern Science.* Edited by Sidney Hook. New York: Collier Books, 1961.

Hume, David. *A Treatise of Human Nature.* Edited by L. A. Selby-Bigge. Oxford: Clarendon Press, 1888.

James, William. "Does 'Consciousness' Exist?" *Essays in Radical Empiricism and a Pluralistic Universe.* New York: Longmans Green, 1943.

Kenny, Anthony. *Action, Emotion and Will.* London: Routledge & Kegan Paul; New York: Humanities Press, 1963.

Lewis, H. D. "Mind and Body—Some Observations on Mr. Strawson's Views." *Proceedings of the Aristotelian Society,* 63 (1962–63): 1–22.

Locke, Don. *Myself and Others: A Study in Our Knowledge of Minds.* London: Clarendon Press of Oxford University Press, 1968.

Locke, John. *An Essay Concerning Human Understanding.* Annotated by Alexander Campbell Fraser. 2 vols. New York: Dover Publications, 1959.

Malcolm, Norman. "Three Lectures on Memory." *Knowledge and Certainty.* Englewood Cliffs, N.J.: Prentice-Hall, 1963.

Martin, C. B., and Deutscher, Max. "Remembering." *Philosophical Review,* 75, no. 2 (April 1966): 161–96.

Moore, G. E. *Philosophical Studies.* Totowa, N.J.: Littlefield, Adams, 1965.

Nowell-Smith, P. H. *Ethics.* London: Penguin Books, 1954.

Penelhum, Terence. "Hume on Personal Identity." *Human Understanding: Studies in the Philosophy of David Hume.* Edited by Alexander Sesonske and Noel Fleming. Belmont, Calif.: Wadsworth Publishing Co., 1965.

————. "Personal Identity." *Encyclopedia of Philosophy.* Vol. 6.

————. "Personal Identity, Memory, and Survival." *Journal of Philosophy,* 56, no. 22 (October 1959): 882—903.

Pitcher, George. "Necessitarianism." *Philosophical Quarterly,* 2 (1961): 201—12.

Plantinga, Alvin. *God and Other Minds: A Study of the Rational Justification of Belief in God.* Ithaca, N.Y.: Cornell University Press, 1967.

Powell, Betty. "Uncharacteristic Actions." *Mind,* 68 (1959): 492—509.

Pucetti, Roland. *Persons: A Study of Possible Moral Agents in the Universe.* London: Macmillan, 1968.

Quinton, Anthony. "The Soul." *Journal of Philosophy,* 59, no. 15 (July 1962): 393—409.

Russell, Bertrand. *The Analysis of Mind.* London: George Allen & Unwin, 1921; New York: Macmillan, 1921.

————. "On the Nature of Acquaintance." *Logic and Knowledge: Essays.* Edited by Robert Charles Marsh. New York: Macmillan, 1956.

Ryle, Gilbert. *The Concept of Mind.* New York: Barnes & Noble, 1949.

Schmitt, Richard. "Phenomenology." *Encyclopedia of Philosophy.* Vol. 6.

Shaffer, Jerome. "Persons and Their Bodies." *Philosophical Review,* 75, no. 1 (January 1966): 59—77.

————. "Recent Work on the Mind-Body Problem." *American Philosophical Quarterly,* 2, no. 2 (April 1965): 81—104.

Shoemaker, Sydney S. "Personal Identity and Memory." *Journal of Philosophy,* 56, no. 22 (October 1959): 868—82.

————. "Persons and Their Pasts." *American Philosophical Quarterly,* 7, no. 4 (October 1970): 269—85.

————. *Self-Knowledge and Self-Identity.* Ithaca, N.Y.: Cornell University Press, 1963.

————. "Self-reference and Self-awareness." *Journal of Philosophy,* 65, no. 19 (October 3, 1968): 555—67.

Skinner, B. F. "Freedom and the Control of Men." *American Scholar,* 25 (Winter 1955/56): 47—65.

————. *Beyond Freedom and Dignity.* New York: Bantam/Vintage, 1972.

————. *Science and Human Behavior.* New York: Macmillan, 1953.

Solomon, Philip, et al., eds. *Sensory Deprivation: A Symposium Held at Harvard Medical School.* Cambridge, Mass.: Harvard University Press, 1961.

Squires, Roger. "Memory Unchained." *Philosophical Review,* 78, no. 2 (April 1969): 178—96.

Strawson, P. F. *Individuals: An Essay in Descriptive Metaphysics.* Garden City, N.Y.: Doubleday, 1959.

Taylor, Richard. "How to Bury the Mind-Body Problem." *American Philosophical Quarterly,* 6, no. 2 (April 1969): 136—43.

Williams, B. A. O. "Personal Identity and Individuation." *Essays in Philosophical Psychology,* Edited by Donald F. Gustafson. Garden City, N.Y.: Doubleday, 1964.

Woods, Michael. "Reference and Self-Identification." *Journal of Philosophy,* 65, no. 19 (October 3, 1968): 568—78.

X, Malcolm. *The Autobiography of Malcolm X.* Assisted by Alex Haley. New York: Grove Press, 1965.

Special Reference Work

Edwards, Paul, ed. *Encyclopedia of Philosophy*. 8 vols. New York: Macmillan Company and The Free Press, 1967; London: Collier-Macmillan, 1967.

Author Index

Subject Index